Unforgettable Stories

for Young Women

About Love, Hope,

and Happiness

A FIRESIDE BOOK
Published by Simon & Schuster
New York   London   Toronto   Sydney   Singapore

CHOCOLATE
for a
TEEN'S
HEART

KAY ALLENBAUGH

FIRESIDE
Rockefeller Center
1230 Avenue of the Americas
New York, NY 10020

FIRESIDE and colophon are registered trademarks
of Simon & Schuster, Inc.

Manufactured in the United States of America

1   3   5   7   9   10   8   6   4   2

Library of Congress Cataloging-in-Publication Data
Chocolate for a teen's heart : unforgettable stories for young women
about love, hope, and happiness / [compiled by] Kay Allenbaugh.
            p.   cm.
1. Teenage girls—Conduct of life.   2. Young women—Conduct of life.
                I. Allenbaugh, Kay.
                BJ1651.C47   2001
158.2'0835'2—dc21   200102810

ISBN 0-7432-1380-7

o Sheri Terjeson, who has

gracefully overcome challenges

to find love

and happiness in her life

CONTENTS

III

IF THE SHOE FITS

IV

DOING MY OWN DANCE

V

PATHWAYS

INTRODUCTION

*L*ove. *It's what young women think about most. Like* finding and keeping good friends, sorting and sifting with Mom and Dad, playing with a favorite pet, and entering the exciting but uncertain world of romance. In *Chocolate for a Teen's Heart*, women and girls from all walks of life share their own true stories of first love, heartbreak, happiness, and gratitude for all the different kinds of lasting love in their lives.

At no other time is it more important to have the reassurance that we are not alone than in our teen years. They are sometimes difficult, filled with bittersweet but often delicious longing and hope for a special romantic love and friends with whom we can share our deepest secrets. These true tales—whether they are about the agony of waiting for an invitation to the prom, the ecstasy of first love, the recollection of our most embarrassing moment, or the unexpected twists and turns of friendships—capture the emotional roller coaster we all face as teenagers. These storytellers will warm your heart as they reveal how they tested boundaries, pushed the limits as far as they could go, and ultimately learned to cherish those things they hold most dear.

Share these pages with friends and family, one at a time, or all at once. They will serve as a road map as you seek love and happiness in your own life. Funny and poignant, sweet and delicious, *Chocolate for a Teen's Heart* will have you laughing and crying as you read each storyteller's journey, and cheering as she ultimately comes out on top.

I
OUR TEACHERS COME IN MANY FORMS

The most beautiful thing in the world is, precisely,
the conjunction of learning and inspiration.

WANDA LANDOWSKA

MUDDY KISSES

*y boyfriend, Alex, and I have this ongoing argu-
ment about kissing.* The other day he overheard me
gossiping with a friend about her first kiss. At one
point, I had asked her, "Did he kiss you, or did you kiss him?" I
considered it a rather normal question for the situation. Alex, on
the other hand, had been absolutely floored.

"What's the difference?" he demanded of me later. I attempted
to explain, but it didn't work at all. Then I tried to tell him how it
was a complicated process that, being a guy, he just couldn't understand. He didn't seem to like that answer either and has been
bugging me about it ever since.

Today, Alex and I went on a picnic in a little park in the hills. It
was the first genuinely sunny day we've had in a long time, and he
and I were not the only ones out enjoying it. We sat at a table in
the shade of a big oak tree. Our table overlooked a muddy green
field where about six big guys were roughing out a game of foot-
ball. For a while, we amused ourselves with watching them.

It was a very loud and animated game. At one point, the rowdi-
est of the guys leapt up to grab the ball and landed flat on his back
in a huge hole of mud. Everything was quiet for a moment. Then
with a sudden burst of hysterical laughter, he threw his arms back
into the mud and began smearing it all over himself.

I was aghast. "Why in the world did he do that?" I wondered
aloud. The guy was now back up and in the game, completely
covered in brown muck.

"What do you mean?" Alex asked, looking at me as though I

had questioned why the sky was blue. "Haven't you ever played contact sports after it has rained?"

"Well, yes, but if I ever landed in a mud puddle, I wouldn't roll in it just to make sure it got everywhere." I was shocked at such an absurd idea. "Why?" I asked, a thought suddenly popping into my head. "Would *you*?"

There was a long pause while Alex pondered the question seriously. "Well," he finally responded in a slow, patient voice, "it's kind of like your kissing thing."

BRIANNA MAHIN-AYERS

*Infatuation is fleeting desire—one set
of glands calling to another.*
ANN LANDERS

QUITTING TIME

*T*he social rules at St. Joseph's seemed pretty simple. If you were sick of your boyfriend, you told him,
"It's quits." Of course, the very same thing could happen to you if your boyfriend became sick of you. Once you had
been "quitted," you assumed the role of tragic heroine of the
week in your group of girlfriends.

Some weeks, it was almost a contest to see whose heart was
most broken. Still, recovery from these breakups tended to be relatively quick. My cousin Kate—two years and six months older
than I—loved to inform me that things would get more complicated once sex came into the picture. She was as much a virgin as
I, but she knew lots about relationships from reading all the magazines in her mom's hair salon.

I officially entered the dating scene the week before Easter
break. Somewhere around Holy Thursday or Good Friday, I fell
madly in love with Jay Cilentello. I couldn't stop thinking about
him—even checked our astrological compatibility in Kate's *Cosmo*
guide. I had already made my feelings clear on the class grapevine
when I received a note on torn loose-leaf from Jay asking me to go

out with him. Even though it was understood that most of us were not really allowed to go out on real dates, having a boyfriend definitely made lunchtime and recess more exciting. I sent back my "Yes" on the back of the note, signing my name inside of a heart to signify my commitment. I looked at his unusually clear face as he read my response and blinked at him, since I could not wink.

Jay and I started dating at school. We held hands under the tables in the library, had long, serious talks at recess, and exchanged relatively dry kisses during slide shows in the science lab. Almost all of my girlfriends were happy for me. Sarah Cunningham even said that she thought Jay and I made a really cute couple. This was the ultimate compliment. The only person who made rude comments was Jennifer Grant, who, with her perfect, long blond hair and position as leader of our grade's most powerful clique, often looked and acted like the villain in a television after-school special.

One morning I overheard her saying that Jay was using me because I was easy. It's hard to shake off those kinds of words, even when you're still a virgin. I went up to Jennifer after social studies class and told her that she'd better stop talking trash about me— or else. I'd never really fought anyone before, but I figured I'd probably be able to at least pull out some of her hair if the need arose. Seemingly unimpressed with my threats, Jennifer pranced off without saying a word. The two girls who served as her lackeys followed her down the hall giggling and whispering behind their hands.

"You need a makeover," Kate said over the phone that evening, between crunches of her carrot and celery snacks. "It will boost your confidence and help you learn to deal with complex social situations." Kate believed in salvation in the form of "before and after" photos. Not having any better ideas, I ran over to her house to see what changes she was proposing. I started to lose my nerve when I saw all the pages she had torn out from her collection of magazines. After all, the idea was to show that I was not easy. Kate promised that I would look sophisticated, not trampy. She also told me all the tips she knew on how to keep a man. Over the previous several months, Kate had collected about thirty pages on this one topic alone.

The next morning I followed Kate's prescription to the letter. I had even let her trim my hair a little and fixed it in the style we had seen on three cover girls. More important than the physical transformation was the new set of principles I had absorbed from the advice in the "problem page" of various magazines. I was going to be a new woman—smart, carefree, independent. As I walked into homeroom, the first thing I saw was Jay talking to Jennifer. Their conversation was intense. I could tell by the way she kept pushing her hair behind her ears—and the way his eyes followed her as she did. I refused to ruin my new eyeliner and held my tears as I walked over to my desk. I pretended not to see them, which worked out fine since they didn't seem to notice me.

As the first morning bell rang, we all sat in our seats and waited for our teacher to address us. She came in the room and called on Jennifer, who was still whispering to the girl behind her.

"Jennifer, would you like to share whatever is so important with the whole class?" said Ms. Carey.

"Oh excuse me, Ms. Carey," said Jennifer with eyes open wide and guiltless. "I was just wondering why she had so much makeup on." I hung my head when I realized that *she* was me.

The class giggled. Of course. Two idiot boys in the back row stomped their feet. It took another ten minutes just to finish roll call. I kept staring at my desk trying to hide my red face. This was social homicide. I had just dropped down on the popularity scales to the ranks of nose pickers and farters. Unfair, but true.

I heard a familiar masculine cough, and finally looked up, thinking that maybe a little comfort was forthcoming. I raised my eyes just in time to see Jay across the room mouthing the words, "It's quits." So much for Cousin Kate's magazines, the new eyeliner, and attitude with a capital "A"—I knew this was going to hurt for a while.

BRIDGET LOPEZ

Two years ago in Los Angeles I met my college roommate for the first time. There she was standing at the curb near our dorm: tall, slender, with long dark hair, looking absolutely perfect. And there I was: sweating in the unfamiliar heat, standing next to my mother with her tear-drenched face, an array of disorganized luggage at my feet. My roommate was from Southern California, but she looked like she'd just stepped out of an Amazon forest with her exotic good looks, and I could barely peel my sticky, flattened hair off of the side of my face.

As we sat in our room and looked through her modeling portfolio, my pictures from back home of my family and friends began to wane in importance, taking on a rather dull existence on the edge of my desk. I looked at pictures of her acting and theater performances, and my dreams of being a screenwriter did not seem so fantastic anymore, since I had nothing to show for them. My roommate told me she had a boyfriend in town and that she'd be spending evenings at his house, but would check in with me during the day to say hi and do some studying.

He had lots of money and took her to the finest restaurants and nightclubs in L.A. My nights were filled with lounging around with girls in the dorm, spending time on the Internet, and if I was lucky, watching a good movie. Her stories of meeting celebrities in VIP rooms and being whirled around in a world of fine food and beautiful people produced in me a subconscious yearning for her life.

Sometimes we'd drive around in her brand-new maroon Jetta, since I didn't have a car. During these times together, I couldn't help but feel that she was somehow on this higher plane, and I kept forgetting that she was my age.

She drove me to a dentist appointment one day, and she looked so confident. Her hair blew in the breeze as she held her arm out the window and put her pencil-thin leg up on the seat as she careened around the streets with familiarity. She blew me a kiss goodbye after dropping me off, reminding me of a famous movie star.

Many times I'd find five of her friends laughing and talking when I'd come into our room. I would leave or sit at the computer and work online. She tried to incorporate me into conversations, but they were "drama people," I thought, and I didn't understand them.

Over the weeks, her "niceness" was just too much for me. Near as I could tell, she knew everyone on campus, and they all loved her. Her amount of greatness seemed to equal the measure of my loneliness and anxiety about being in this foreign land of Los Angeles. Her boyfriend was also too perfect. He had the good looks of an actor and treated her really well. He was in love with her, and I was green with envy.

On a particularly hot, sweaty day in mid-September, I had just flunked the first test of my entire life and received a "C" on a paper I'd spent the whole night before writing and editing. I was in the worst mood ever and grateful for some time alone in our room. When the phone rang, I debated whether to answer it, since it was usually for her. I paused for a second then got it in case I'd won the lottery, or it was Leonardo di Caprio finally responding to the fan mail I'd sent him.

My best friend from home was calling. What a relief! Finally to hear a familiar voice. I missed her so much, and we immediately drowned in the comfort of each other's woes. I shared with her my horrible day and how I'd barely made any friends. As I went on and on, my situation seemed to get more pathetic, and I looked over at my roommate's pictures of all of her friends, and began to get even more envious of her. My life seemed to really be in the depths of doom, while my roommate had everything going her way.

I began to talk about her. I don't know if it was to make me feel better, or just because I was so jealous, but I went on a whole tirade about how I couldn't stand my roommate. I told my friend that my roommate was stupid, phony, and fake, and that she couldn't even act (I had never actually seen her act). Nothing could stop me, and it seemed like I just kept on reeling off terrible nonsensical things about her and her boyfriend.

Suddenly I was startled by a rustling sound in the upper bunk. To my horror, I turned and saw my roommate coming down from her bed. I dropped the phone and began to gasp, knowing that she'd heard my every negative word. Her face had a look of dark despair from the hurt I'd inflicted. My heart sank. I had never felt so guilty, horrible, and disgusting in my entire life. She tearfully whispered, "I have to go to class," and ran out of the room. She had obviously been napping up in her bed, and I hadn't seen or noticed her thin body up against the wall.

I spent the whole day crying and drowning in my own misery and guilt. I couldn't believe how badly I'd put my foot in my mouth! There was nothing I could say or do to make her listen to me after that day. I wrote her a five-page letter and put it in her desk, knowing that she'd probably never read it. I immediately volunteered to move out and quickly made myself invisible to her and her friends. I became reclusive, hanging out with only one other person.

Since then, my old roommate and I have never talked and have never so much as exchanged glances. If we see each other coming across campus, we usually just both walk in opposite directions.

Now, as I sit here in my Level One acting class nearly two years later, trying to learn the basic tenets of the skill, I reflect back and ask myself, *Who was I actually talking about on the phone that fateful day—her or me?* I've discovered the hard way that when I see things in others I don't like or find fault with, they are only reflections of the negative things I don't like about myself.

When I think of this experience now, the word *karma* comes to mind—the law of cause and effect from our actions in a lifetime that produce favorable or unfavorable results in the future. If it's remotely possible that we have more than one life, I think I've burned off one hundred years of negative karma in working through this one!

I'm not the same person I was two years ago. What I do now is say only good things about other people. It always puts them in a better light, and it gives me peace of mind—something I missed dearly during the last couple of years while recovering from "hoof-in-mouth" disease.

KIMBERLY BIRKLAND

THE SUMMER OF THE BLUE BOMBER

On the first day of summer vacation, I approached the stone steps of Porter Convalescent Center with a mixture of trepidation and excitement. The Saturday before, I had attended junior volunteer orientation there. Now I was a full-fledged "Cheery Blossom." I straightened my bright pink smock and marched inside. I felt like Florence Nightingale, striding into battle to heal and hearten the troops.

The volunteer director assigned me to 3 South. As we rode the rickety elevator, she explained that this was a long-term care unit. Most of its patients would never go home. My stomach lurched as we opened the door to 3 South. The stench of urine and Lysol overwhelmed me. The head nurse, Ms. Ticknor, was less than welcoming.

"Sit in there and don't get underfoot until I see what I can do with you," she said, nodding to a conference room.

Half an hour passed before Ms. Ticknor and another nurse came in and flopped at the table.

"You," she said, glaring at my nametag, "Kathy, is it? Go down to 311 and see what Miss Blume wants."

The other nurse laughed. "Have mercy, Tick! Don't send the kid in to the Blue Bomber."

I stopped. "The Blue Bomber?"

They laughed.

"Just duck when you go in," Ms. Ticknor said. "And don't take anything she says personally. Just see what she wants and get out."

The light over 311 flashed ominously. I knocked timidly. When no one answered, I pushed open the door. A silver pitcher barely missed my head as it smashed into the wall, splattering water and ice.

Miss Blume was smaller than me. Blueberry-tinted hair fanned her head like an ancient string mop. She uttered every curse word I had ever heard as she scrambled about for something else to throw.

"Whaddya want, girlie?" she screamed. "Where's Ticknor? Don't stand there staring, get out of here!"

I can't say exactly what came over me, but I suddenly felt very angry—angry with Ms. Ticknor, angry with Miss Blume, and especially angry with Florence Nightingale for misleading me in her biographies. Everything I'd learned at orientation about communicating with the patients left my mind.

"It's no big thrill for me to be in here, either," I said.

My words shocked me. I was about to apologize when something strange happened. Miss Blume stopped shouting. She stopped scrambling and looked straight at me. Then she laughed. She laughed and laughed and laughed.

"Come here, girlie," she said at last. "Come here, you sassy thing."

I shuffled to her bedside and tried not to cringe when she pressed her gnarled hand over mine.

"I . . . I came to see what you want," I stammered.

Miss Blume snorted. "What I want, you can't get me, girlie. I suppose I just wanted Ticknor to come in so I could aggravate her. No sense in feeling aggravated if I can't pass it on."

I smiled. "Want some more ice water?"

Miss Blume smiled back. Her eyes twinkled. I cleaned up the water and brought a fresh pitcher of ice water into 311. I was surprised to see that Miss Blume had made an effort to tame her hair.

"Want me to fix your hair?" I asked.

She shrugged. "It's not fixable."

I took a brush from her drawer and worked the blue strands

into a modified French braid. I found a scarf in her locker and tied it on the end of the braid. I propped up the mirror on her bed table. She stared at herself for a moment, then at me.

"Not bad," she said. "What's your name?"

"Kathy."

"What are you, about thirteen?"

"I'll be fourteen next month."

She grunted. There was a long silence.

"Want me to read to you?" I asked, picking up an old gardening magazine.

She grabbed it from me.

"Some fool volunteer left that," she said, throwing it off the bed. "Do I look like Old MacDonald? What do I know from gardening?"

I laughed. I looked around the dingy room. There were no photographs. The only visible personal item was a small, exquisite silver clock. *Who was Miss Blume?* I wondered.

"I used to read," Miss Blume was saying. "Read a lot of novels."

I thought about the novel I was reading from my summer list.

"I can bring one," I offered. 'It's kind of—well, kind of bad in parts. It's *Catcher in the Rye.* Do you want me to bring it tomorrow?"

"Yeah, sure, if you want," Miss Blume said. But she didn't sound like she believed that I would.

Throughout the rest of the summer, Miss Blume and I laughed and cried our way through *Catcher in the Rye.* Miss Blume chuckled out loud at teenager Holden Caulfield's attempts to survive in an adult world. She clucked over his profanity and cheered his concern for his little sister, Phoebe.

In between chapters, Miss Blume shared some of herself. I learned that she had never married. She worked her adult life as a salesclerk in a department store. The rest of her time had been spent caring for her mother. After her mother died, the previous year, Miss Blume had sold their house and furnishings to finish paying for her mother's funeral and medical bills. That did not anger her. What did upset her was that just after she paid the last bill, she was diagnosed with terminal cancer.

We finished *Catcher in the Rye* during my last week at Porter. Mom and I had decided I would not volunteer during the upcoming school year, since it was my freshman year at high school and I had a lot of adjustments to make. It was hard saying goodbye to Miss Blume. She patted my cheek and asked me to come back during winter break. I promised I would. Even Ms. Ticknor hugged me and said how much she would miss me.

By October, I had become so immersed in high school life that Porter seemed a vague memory. Then one evening Ms. Ticknor called. She asked if I could come to see Miss Blume. It sounded urgent.

Miss Blume looked smaller than ever. I had to get very close to hear her voice.

"I didn't want to wait till winter break," she said. Her eyes still twinkled. "I want you to take this clock. It's the only thing I kept of Mom's. I don't want old Ticknor to get it."

I swallowed hard. The clock barely filled the palm of my hand.

"I'll treasure it," I said.

Miss Blume put her hand on mine.

"Thanks," she whispered. "You and Phoebe and Holden made all the difference."

I left Porter with the clock tucked in my coat pocket. As I walked to Dad's car, the clock's muffled ticking reminded me of the fragility of life. I thought ahead to next summer, and wondered if I would be lucky enough to encounter another Blue Bomber.

KATHLEEN M. MULDOON

SOUL REVIVAL

*T*he wind was so raw that we kept moving so our hands and feet wouldn't go numb. Gusts whipped sideways the giant wreaths connected to lampposts above our heads and forced the town to huddle closer together. In spite of the weather, everyone grinned in anticipation of the Wake Forest Christmas Parade.

The crowd lined the streets four and five people deep. The smaller kids who came with us had hatched a secret plan on the ride over and vowed to fill their pockets full of candy thrown from the floats. When they heard the distant tiny sounds of Christmas music, they wormed their way to the curb. My girls, like any decent teenagers, moved away from me and pretended not to know me.

The leader of the parade was a twenty-piece band from the Lilly Parks Christian School. They played "Oh Come All Ye Faithful." After them, future ballet stars from Miss June's Dance Academy performed a jerky Hokey Pokey. Tiny sweatsuit-clad dancers all moving to their own steps. None of them in time to the music. A collective "Ahh" gently sounded through the crowd.

Solemn Boy Scouts in full uniform marched by. The older boys' eyes said they would rather be anywhere else hanging out and acting cool. A younger scout reached our spot and threw all his candy high in the air. He was almost trampled by hordes of candy-grabbing kids.

Junior Miss Wake Forest rode by and regally surveyed her kingdom in a Corvette convertible. Following close behind was

Miss Teen Wake County. Lovely little snow queens with big hair, tiaras, and blue eye shadow, all wrapped up in thick, white fur coats. Their practiced waves had lost some pep by the time they reached us.

The Wake Forest High School band marched by and their knees threatened to touch the sky. A methodical drill team waved red and black flags, as baton twirlers in their shorts and tights threw, whirled, and spun around. The band played "Joy to the World," their faces screwed up with concentration. Their black and red uniforms made them look like life-size toy soldiers.

The Centerville City Car Club was six old men in ancient cars that snaked along with back seats filled with children hanging out the windows—grandkids, church kids, and probably a few borrowed neighborhood kids.

Keystone Kops on minibikes chased a striped prisoner around and around in circles. Countless sparkling floats were loaded down with red-and-green-clad employees and their families. The fire department's new engine was covered with Santas, and when the driver blasted his horn, one brave Santa climbed down the side ladder.

Drums as loud as thunder made the first row of onlookers step into the street and crane their necks to see where the sound was coming from. Two tall African-American teenagers marched toward us carrying a black-and-gold banner, which read "Helping Friends Mission." The flag bearers behind them were dressed in silky black suits, with long capes and enormous top hats. They carried five-foot-long poles topped with gold flags and pumped their legs high in the air as they furiously waved their flags. They reminded me of dazzling dancers from the Mardi Gras parade.

The music of the group consisted of twenty drummers, who pounded their instruments so hard I thought the sides would burst. Between those groups was a dance troupe. Black girls aged ten to eighteen dressed in halter tops, and black hot pants, with gold sequins dotting their entire bodies.

A woman in a leather jacket to my left said, "There go my tax dollars. They can dance, but not work."

Her companion replied, "They sure don't look like they have missed any meals to me."

My girls made their way to my side when the comments got nastier.

"Who is responsible for this?" the woman asked.

A slightly overweight girl of about eleven danced closest to us. Her hair was piled high with gold studs woven into a mass of braids. A man in front of me held up his half-eaten hot dog and shouted, "Hey girl! I'm finished with this. You want it?" She beamed at him as his children doubled over with laughter.

Disgusted with the comments, I told my girls, "Let's go," and started to leave when I saw the other dancers part as the girl moved toward the center of the street. The drummers began a song with a slower beat. All the other dancers stopped. The girl smiled at the people and walked in a circle. She held her arms above her head and began shaking her hips. When she began rapid leg movements and elaborate hand gestures, she all but merged with the music. Her thick braids swung and snapped in the sunlight. She became a blur of black, gold, and light.

The drums got louder until I could feel the beat on my skin. The crowd fell silent as this perfect creature the color of onyx transported us to an ancient time when melting one's soul with the beat of a drum was holy. Her movements seemed effortless, the smile never left her face, but I noticed she was shiny with sweat, and her eyes shone bright with determination. It wasn't an angry dance, but a dance that said, "I am beautiful. Watch me. Just watch me."

When she finished her dance, the girl bowed first to one side of the street, then turned and bowed in our direction. The whole street was silent as the girl resumed her place in line. Then the crowd exploded with applause. They jumped, clapped, and shouted, "Yes! Yes!" The girl turned and smiled again at the man who had offered her his hot dog and moved on down the street.

My heart pounded in my brain. I barely remembered the rest of the parade or when we walked back to the car. That was the bravest thing I had ever witnessed. My youngest was quiet until the car warmed, and then she said, "Mama, when I grow up, I want to be a dancer."

LEIGH SENTER

I have come to understand that every day
is something to cherish.
KERRI STRUG

HAVING OURSELVES
A GENTLE DAY

Iwoke up with a smile on that morning at the farm. It was July, I was seven, and while every day at my grandparents' farm in Turkey Knob, Pennsylvania, was a special one, today promised even more. As kids, we always had summer vacations at the farm. All of us grandchildren visited in pairs or groups of three or four, sorted according to age, gender, and temperament.

This morning, for the first time I was here with no siblings or cousins along. My older sister had left for her first trip to summer camp two days before, and my parents had deposited me on the farm in an attempt to ease my jealous pain. I woke up pain-free, knowing that for the next few days my grandma and grandpap were mine alone.

We led a charmed life as kids on the farm, where work and play merged, where everything was homegrown and homemade, where the backyard felt like it went on forever, and where we slopped hogs, chased chickens, churned butter, and used cow plops for first base.

I hit the kitchen and downed two bowls of oatmeal with home-canned peaches on top. The night before, I'd run to the cellar and brought up two quart jars, one of peaches and the other of home-made applesauce—the kind with apples still in big chunks. My grandpap finished his own breakfast, picked a quick basket of raspberries, and took off for the lower place to check on the live-stock and then for town. He said he'd be back for dinner.

Grandma and I put our bowls in the sink and I asked, "What do we do this morning?" That was every morning's question after breakfast at the farm. Work came first and began right after break-fast. But today when I asked, Grandma's response was one I'd never heard. She sat down, put both hands flat on the kitchen table, smiled big, and said, "Whatever we want." I looked at her and knew she meant it! She explained that she'd already gathered the eggs and fed the hogs. "We'll have to milk this evening, of course. But till then," she said, "you and I'll have ourselves a gen-tle day."

We grabbed two fishing poles and left them leaning against the fence at the top of the yard. Then we walked. We walked slowly and held hands while Grandma talked to me. She told me her sto-ries, some I'd always known and some I'd never heard. She told me that my grandpap had helped build the far wall on the barn when he was a very little boy and that my daddy had repaired the same wall when he was only nine. She pointed to an overgrown lane where she and Grandpap had been stranded in the snow on their way home the day they were married. She showed me the old wooden kitchen table, now discarded in a shed, where both my grandpap and my daddy had been born.

We sat on a fence that looked down on the farm, and she pointed to the field where a one-room schoolhouse used to stand. We lay in the grass and watched cloud pictures and then we rolled down the hill. First I asked if she was able. She stood up and stretched to the sky with drama and groans. Then she bent from the waist and grabbed her shoes. "Yep," she teased. "If I'm still able to touch my toes, I'm able to roll down this hill!"

We rolled and rolled, and at the bottom, she showed me where a swarm of hornets had chased my daddy and my aunt Ellen one summer day and another spot where my grandpap had chased my daddy and my aunt Doris for riding the plow horses bareback. We found honeysuckle and sucked our fill, and picked wildflowers for our hair.

At some point, we found ourselves back at the gate where we'd left the fishing poles. We picked them up and headed toward the pond. I knew which rocks to turn over for worms, and in short order we had three bluegills each. We ambled slowly up the long lane to the house, and I listened some more—not just to Grandma but to every sound of that summer day.

We fried the fish, boiled little red potatoes, and opened my jar of applesauce. When we finished, Grandpap was home. After dinner, we went out to the sunny afternoon porch. Grandpap opened the brown bag he'd come home with and presented each of us with our own pint container of Dairy Queen soft ice cream! We talked and laughed, and I moaned when my giggles made my too full stomach ache, and we laughed even harder and then ate some more.

We found shade after dinner and rested. When I woke up, the sun was falling, and I stretched to see Grandma waiting on the porch. "Ready?" She asked. I took her hand, and we headed to the barn. The cows were waiting for us and so were the barn cats. I asked why she always filled the barn cats' bowls first. She smiled and said that the first milk goes to the felines, because they're kind enough to let us use their house to milk our cows.

Back in the kitchen, Grandma taught me how to hide the dirty dinner dishes in the oven when night is almost here and there are lightning bugs to be caught. I fell asleep with a jar of the bugs for a nightlight on the table by my bed. While I slept, they were set free and the jar with air holes in its lid was put back under the porch step until the next time.

Years later, with babies of my own, it's my turn to teach my grandma's lesson. It's my turn to share a gentle day—filled with playing and visiting and feasting and snoozing—a day when we feel loved, happy, well fed, and content.

Grandma taught me how wonderful it is to sometimes move easily and peacefully through time, away from the hard work of everyday living. To live for a little while at a sweeter level, where every bit of the day is just right because wherever I am is the best place to be.

Today, right after breakfast I'm going to take the hands of someone I love and begin slowly. I've promised myself that not once during today will I say that it's time to get started or move on or finish up. We'll begin feeling just right, because we'll be having ourselves a gentle day.

ELLEN DURR

A good time to laugh is any time you can.

LINDA ELLERBEE

BULLY FOR WHO?

A s an only child growing up in suburban Atlanta in
the late 1950s and early '60s, I loved visiting my cousin in
northern Georgia. Linda lived on a farm and was my
best friend, the sister I never had.

The summer Linda turned sixteen, I was still fifteen. She was allowed to date, but I (not having reached that magical age) would
have to wait until December.

That seemed eons away, so we dreamed up a way to double-
date. After everyone was asleep, we'd sneak out of the house and
meet two local boys Linda knew. Later, we'd sneak back in. Great
plan!

We congratulated ourselves on our ingenuity. On the ap-
pointed night, we retired early, which should have been an immediate tip-off to Aunt Mary Nell. We were wearing good clothes
under our nightgowns. We lay sweating on the iron poster beds
until Mama Sewell and Aunt Mary Nell were sound asleep.

At her signal, I raised Linda's bedroom window for her to climb
through. She tore her new capri pants and used a swear word. Fortunately, Aunt Mary Nell's rhythmic snoring reassured us that all
was still well.

We sneaked to the gate separating the property from an adjoining farm owned by our uncle Roy and aunt Margaret. Linda lifted the latch and stepped through.

Swatting at an insect circling my head, I let the gate slam against the fence post with a thunderous crash. We strained our eyes against the darkness and were relieved not to see any house lights come on.

Just at that moment we heard a rumbling in the bushes. Someone or something brushed past us. Something very large with wiry hair and hot breath!

Then the awful truth hit. "Oh no! Horatio is out!" gasped Linda. "We've got to put him back."

We chased Uncle Roy's prize bull in the moonlight. Linda yelled, "Catch his head! Hold him!" But there was no way that I— a city girl—was going to grab that bull's head.

As we ran, we prayed. Uncle Roy would never forgive us if anything happened to Horatio—he was the best bull in the county.

Finally realizing we'd never catch him, Linda suggested we call Aunt Margaret.

"She'll help us corral him, and she won't squeal either. Aunt Margaret's a pal."

"No," I protested. "We can't tell anyone. My dad will kill me if he gets wind of this. I'll never be able to visit you again."

We exchanged breathless protests until finally we agreed for Linda to sneak back inside and telephone Aunt Margaret. Luckily, Aunt Margaret was still up and alone. When she arrived, she left her truck lights on pointing them in our general direction. Cautiously she approached Horatio.

Suddenly Horatio bolted, and she grabbed his tail as he went by. Aunt Margaret isn't a small woman, but that old bull dragged her around the yard like a rag doll. She was screaming at the top of her lungs, so all the house lights quickly came on.

We were in for it now! I figured my folks would come for me first thing in the morning. I might as well just start packing. Meanwhile, Aunt Margaret's ride continued, through briars and bushes, across plowed fields and over the lawn. Her firm grip held.

Then, unexpectedly, Uncle Roy showed up carrying a little silver whistle. He blew it. Amazingly Horatio stopped dead. He lowered a massive head and trotted up to Uncle Roy like a pet retriever.

After prying Aunt Margaret's ten-finger death grip off Horatio's tail, Uncle Roy led him back through the gate and into the barn. Meanwhile, we helped Aunt Margaret inside picking twigs and burrs off her clothes. While Mama Sewell got her a glass of water, we managed to deposit her in the recliner. Obviously, we never made it to our rendezvous.

Incredibly, my parents never found out about this episode. The question of how Linda and I happened to be outside was never raised. Everyone assumed we'd heard Horatio rumbling around and tried to put him up ourselves. They never questioned that we were wearing our "good" clothes.

For days afterward, we giggled at how funny Aunt Margaret looked holding on to Horatio's tail. We also marveled at Horatio's obedience to Uncle Roy's whistle. Forty years later, Linda and I still laugh about our double date with Horatio T. Bull.

SHEILA S. HUDSON

BUTTERFLY CHARISMA

The way I see it, everyone has at least one story of a victory or triumph over something. For some people it's standing up to a bully, living out an incredibly challenging dream, or finding the courage to say no under peer pressure. My story is one of a butterfly. Not just any ordinary butterfly . . . he's beautiful.

Last year, I was fourteen and a freshman in high school. I was a little lonely. I didn't really know anyone except a few girls who graduated from junior high a year before me. Also, I looked older than my classmates. I sat in homeroom for what seemed to be the longest hour of my life before we received program cards. The class periods were shortened that day so we could just get a feel for our classmates and our teachers. Annoyed that my relaxing summer vacation was over, I really didn't care for either until fourth period, Spanish. That's when I noticed him. He was tall with curly hair, light smooth skin, and the cutest smile.

Sixth period, lunch, came quickly, and I sat with those older girls. I quietly listened to their puppy-love boyfriend stories as I scribbled little poems and riddles onto my napkin. I looked up and there he was again. He entered the lunchroom saying hi to all of his male friends and what appeared to be the large sum of girls with crushes on him.

"Adrian, who is that?"

"Who?"

"That guy!" I said with my eyes beaming directly toward him.

"That's Bobby. He's cute, right?"

I tried to act like I didn't agree. "He's all right."

"Every girl in this school, almost every girl he's ever met, likes him or once did. That includes me."

I kept thinking he looked like someone I knew, so I asked, "What's his last name?"

"Lawrence. Bobby Lawrence."

I thought to myself, *I know the Lawrence family*. It was probably the biggest family of cousins, aunts, uncles, and grandchildren in the state of New York. I had probably seen Bobby before and hadn't even realized it.

We started talking after Spanish class one day. I think I liked him even more because I got along well with his family. We found things in common. He was a junior. Pretty soon we'd walk toward the park or some place nice, deep in conversation. At first, I worried a lot that Bobby would abandon our friendship for some other girl. A girl with a beautiful smile and better conversation. Innocently, I had opened my heart and become vulnerable.

I learned more about him as time went by. Eventually, I realized there was cause for concern. I watched Bobby slowly disappear from time to time to be with other girls. People labeled him as a heartbreaker, but I began to see him differently. I compared him to a butterfly. Butterflies aren't happy for long after they're captured. They are better off flying around making people happy and eventually flying away. Bobby flew into my life right when I needed him. He landed right in my grasp. I'll never forget how magnificent it was to have had a hold on such a beautiful creature.

Bobby is my story because there are some people who go through life never having experienced true friendship. Never knowing how wonderful it feels to have loved and let go.

I let him fly like a butterfly onto my open palm without closing my hand too tightly around him. I've learned it's important to keep a loose grasp if you want to keep a butterfly around. We are better off that way. Bobby and I have been able to stay close friends through thick and thin. We still have those priceless conversations. Sometimes, hearing his silly laugh gets me through the worst day.

I'm not sure what the future will have in store for us. I don't worry about it anymore. I have time to figure out the complicated stuff, but one thing I'm certain of is our enduring friendship. I wouldn't change a thing. I'm glad we met my freshman year. He's the most beautiful butterfly I know.

NICOLE DOMINIQUE BURGAN

II
GIVING MORE
THAN YOU TAKE

My goal in life is to be the kind of person

my dog thinks I am.

AUTHOR UNKNOWN

SOCCER SATURDAY

*T*he sun shines blindingly. It is a crisp and clear early Saturday morning. Frigid air fills my fifteen-year-old lungs as I gaze around the knobby field with a sense of excitement and expectation for my little Hawks, as I take in the sweet smells of dew and freshly sliced grass. I arrive thirty minutes before game time to prepare for the sport and gaiety that await me.

Slowly, minivans and station wagons inch up to the curb next to the field. Within each family-oriented vehicle is at least one giggling, energetic seven- or eight-year-old girl. A mom and several little athletes pile out of one of the cars, along with Fido, the chocolate Labrador. I have the young soccer stars gather around in a huddle, like I'm collecting a handful of acorns. Their smiling faces beam radiantly up at me in adoration. The girls crane their necks to absorb my words of wisdom. I impart what I think will be helpful from my years of soccer experience and end with encouraging phrases and the thumbs-up sign. They give a high pitched cheer of "Go Hawks!" and squeal with giddiness as they gallop anxiously onto the field to begin the game.

Kick, chase. Kick, chase. *Goal!* Kick, chase. Kick, chase. Uh-oh, goal for the other team. Except, who is counting? It looks like wild mayhem, but to the girls it is instant stardom. For half an hour, they are heroines of the world. They feel triumphant as they may kick a nylon ball through the towering orange flags with the tip of a black leather cleated toe. Their enthusiasm and excitement is contagious as it runs through my veins.

The whistle blows and the game is over. The girls sprint to me with big smiles on their round, pink faces, knowing they have pleased me today. They run to give me big hugs, and I feel their warmth. We give a cheer and then exchange high-fives with the gleeful opponents, because at this innocent level of the sport, everyone is a winner.

A busy mom pulls up and takes out a green plastic Tupperware bowl from the large bag that holds most of her hectic life within. The lid comes off the container and dainty, chubby hands reach in blindly. My girls sink their toothless grins into the sweet and tangy orange pieces to quench their thirst. Sticky fingers wave goodbye, and all the cars drive quickly away. Soon I am left alone.

I pick up the fluorescent orange cones and retrieve the cheap plastic balls. I gaze at one of the more tattered and aged balls, fondly, caressing it with my rough hands. Writing by a faded Sharpie marker states plainly "JUGGLERS," my old team's name from when I was seven. The memories are vivid—eating succulent orange slices and scoring the goals using my tiny cleated toes. The times were so innocent yet powerful. What an impression those years have made on my life—making me strong and sure. I hope to do as well with my little Hawks.

CAROLINE MILLESON

THE BREAKFAST CLUB

*T*he telephone rang into my ninth-grade junior high school classroom. "Jill, please come to the guidance office!" As I walked down the hall, I wondered *why* would someone want *me* to come to the guidance office? As I stepped into the counseling office, I was met by a girl who needed to speak to someone about her friend. I was reassured by the school counselor that I was not in trouble and that someone needed to talk with me. I was called because I was a member of the Breakfast Club.

The Breakfast Club is not a club where one eats breakfast. It is an organization of students started thirteen years ago as a result of a young student's suicide. His mother thought that it could have been prevented had her son talked to someone about how he was feeling.

The B.C., as we call it for short, gives us an opportunity to privately talk to our peers about anything on their minds and in their hearts. Our motto: We care but we don't cure. Members from the previous year, teachers, and counselors select students for the Breakfast Club. The club is a diverse group including, Asians, blacks, whites, athletes, musicians, and students with all levels of academic achievement. The criteria for belonging to the group is to be a good listener, be able to brainstorm ideas, and don't give advice! We barely knew one another in the beginning, but we became fast friends after all the training and experiences we went through.

The call led me to a one-on-one meeting with the girl who had asked me down to the office. It seems that she had found her friend cutting her wrists. I called the counselor into the room because it's important to have an adult involved when a life is in danger, and she took the student out of her classroom.

That's when I met her and found out that she was cutting herself because she didn't care about her life, and thought no one would care if she was gone. She had many problems at home, and recently her grandparents had come to stay with her family. They had made her feel horrible with negative comments directed at her. Her grades weren't the best either, and she didn't get the attention and love she needed at home from her parents.

Just like the boy who had committed suicide years before, she was very good at putting on a happy mask without anyone suspecting that she was depressed. Fortunately, the Breakfast Club was there to help her, confidentially. She and I, and sometimes the counselor, met many times during the year following that phone call to my classroom, and we talked about what was bothering her.

After school was out for the summer, I received a call from her. I asked how her summer was going, and she told me it was great. She had gotten all A's and B's on her report card. Somehow we got into a conversation about popularity. She told me that she was going to be who she wanted to be from now on, and her true friends were the friends that would stick by her no matter what. We also talked about the future and what to expect in high school this fall.

I have a great feeling that I played a positive role in her life. I wasn't an advice giver, but I was someone she could count on to talk with because I listened. I hope I helped her realize that life is definitely worth living. My mom said I made a difference; I say I was just being a friend.

JILL FANCHER

KAY'S TIPS FOR TEENS

1. A lot of nerds grow up to be millionaires.
2. The most important person to be comfortable with is yourself.
3. Solving someone else's problem isn't necessary; listening is enough.
4. You *can* judge a book by its cover. What image do you want to display?
5. Smoking is intriguing—except that it will ruin your skin, yellow your teeth, stain your nails, and ultimately kill you.
6. Pray to your angels; they can help, but only if you ask them to.
7. Be a role model and mentor for someone younger than yourself.
8. Watch a cat relax; cats know how to live in the moment.
9. Observe how a dog adores you; dogs know how to love unconditionally.
10. Choosing to be a passenger in a car with an irresponsible driver is a dumb thing.
11. Being there for others will not only help them but expand your sense of self worth tenfold as well.
12. Decide what's important to you in a relationship, and don't settle for anything less.
13. The way you eat today will affect how you look and feel tomorrow.
14. Be grateful for each new day.
15. Taking one healthy risk a month will build your self-esteem and courage.

16. The older you get, the smarter your mother and father become.

17. Hugging someone each day is good for them and good for you.

18. Give more than you take—it will always come back to you.

19. Remember that every time you are critical of someone else, you are *really* recognizing an aspect of yourself that you don't like.

20. It's always helpful to think things through carefully.

21. You will learn the most from the mistakes you make.

22. If you are patient, you will always find the light at the end of any dark tunnel.

23. Once you decide what you are here to accomplish, picture it and move toward it; doors will open and people will come into your life to support your mission. The universe always supports your soul purpose.

24. Be an observer. You'll learn a lot about people simply by watching.

25. At any given time, you know the right thing to do. Trust yourself completely.

KAY ALLENBAUGH

I was ten years old the first time my sweet, gentle boxer dog Duchess brought me a tiny little package in her big soft lips. It was an infant rabbit with his eyes still closed tight. I felt overwhelmed with the task before me. I was angry with Duchess for confiscating this tiny creature from its natural environment and afraid to watch it die. *What do I do?* I thought, as I stood frozen to the ground in confusion.

My fondness for bunnies began at a very early age, when I received a small green and pink stuffed rabbit as a gift. I never went anywhere without the rabbit. I would carry it, holding its right ear up to my nose and making a noise that sounded almost like purring. It was a security blanket of sorts, and holding on to it made me feel safe.

In my panic it occurred to me that something this real baby bunny needed was to be kept warm and that would be a good first step. So I found a shoebox to make a cozy nest for my new little guest. I shredded lots of soft white Kleenex and created a warm, safe environment for the bunny. That's when I remembered I still had my Tiny Tears dolls that came with miniature baby bottles to fit in a small hole in Tiny Tears' mouth. *This would be perfect for a baby bunny,* I thought—and it was. All right. Within minutes, a plan was beginning to form.

I asked Mom if she had any ideas. She was very skeptical about the prospects of my being able to keep this little one alive and suggested that I speak with the high school biology teacher, Mr. Holtzhauer, who lived directly behind us. He informed me that it would be impossible to raise a wild rabbit for a variety of reasons not the least of which it would be that I couldn't duplicate the mother's milk. He explained baby rabbits would not be able to digest rich cow's milk, which was exactly what I had anticipated feeding my charge. He told me that bunnies needed to be fed frequently, every two to three hours, because they are so small. "Quite honestly, though," he said, "the most humane thing to do is destroy the bunny or have it destroyed."

Well, enough of that kind of advice! I left Mr. Holtzhauer's house with a pit in my stomach and more determination than ever. I decided that I would do whatever it took to help this defenseless bunny survive.

Now what? Well, if cow's milk is too rich, then I'll use skim milk. Mom suggested I add a tiny amount of liquid vitamins to each bottle. I set my alarm and got up every two hours during the night to warm the milk and feed the bunny. During the day, I'd rush home from school at noon and immediately after school to feed the baby rabbit.

To everyone's amazement the bunny was still alive days later, eagerly accepting milk at each feeding, then falling back to sleep while I stroked him. Soon after, the bunny opened his eyes and began hopping around in his box. That's when I began to feed the rabbit grass, lettuce, and carrots. The bunny not only survived, he thrived, and I was hooked.

Over the next several years, my dogs presented me with several more opportunities to repeat this life-affirming exercise, and I eventually raised twelve bunnies that I released in the country once they were ready. Sometime later, Mom and I saw a nature program on television, and we were surprised to learn that female rabbits keep their babies in the nest for a much shorter time than I did before they are left on their own.

It didn't take me long to realize that I have an unusual connection and love for animals. I eventually became a vegetarian when I turned twenty-one, and I've rescued over two hundred animals so far.

Although I'm no longer close to an open field where wild rabbits live, the experience shaped my life forever. For the love of bunnies and the confidence they gave me, I will always create enough space where four-legged ones can come and feel at home.

CINDY POTTER

MISSING THE DANCE

"**W**ould you like to be my date for the ROTC dance?" asked Rick.

I couldn't believe he was asking me. My two best friends had gotten dates weeks ago, so I had given up hope of anyone from ROTC asking me. Rick was the cutest guy in the club! He wanted to go with me? "Are you serious?"

"It's semiformal, so you'll need a dress, but my parents will pay for the tickets and the limo," he responded.

How could I ask for more—a chariot taking Prince Charming and me to the ball? My mouth worded, "Yes," as my heart leapt with joy. I had never been to a semiformal dance before, and now was my chance. This would be the best night of my life!

The moment I got home, I told my mom about Rick's asking. Immediately, she took me shopping to find the perfect dress. We went to the hairdresser's to make an appointment for Friday before the dance to have my hair and nails done. I wanted Rick's eyes to literally pop out of his head when he saw me. I wanted him to take one look at me and fall in love. Could it happen? Would it? Could I be transformed into a beautiful princess?

Before I knew it, days had passed. I couldn't sleep at all. Butterflies fluttered in my stomach, and my head was throbbing. Friday morning I woke up and the whole world seem to spin. I tried to lift my head off the pillow but I couldn't move.

"Honey, you're going to be late for school . . . are you okay?" My mom came into the bedroom. Her hand flew to my forehead. "Oh no! You've got a fever."

I didn't feel hot; I felt cold, so very cold.

My mother helped me dress, and she drove me to my doctor. I had been there only a few minutes before my doctor called an ambulance. I couldn't understand all that my doctor was telling me. All I could hear was a muffled "One-hundred-four-degree fever."

The hospital's bright lighting was blinding as a nurse with long, dark hair stuck two IVs in my arm. I didn't remember seeing her come into my room, only the blanket being thrown on top of me. "Cold, very cold," I said.

"The blanket is filled with ice," she explained. "You have a bad infection. Your doctor ordered fluids and antibiotics for you. Just rest."

I closed my eyes.

It seemed only a few minutes later when I heard, "Good morning." My doctor woke me. "I'm glad you slept through the night. Luckily, we've brought your temperature down. You are one special little girl. You have a very serious ear, nose, and throat infection, but it seems we now have it under control."

"Mom?" I gasped. "Dad?"

"I'm right here." My mother grabbed my hand.

I looked and my parents were there beside me.

"Did I miss the dance?"

My mom smiled. "I called Rick. I got his number out of your address book and let him know that you were in the hospital."

"Oh no!" I cried.

"There'll be other dances," said my doctor. "Be thankful you'll be alive to see them."

Days passed.

I got increasingly stronger and no longer had a temperature. They discovered that I had developed a very bad strep infection that was treated with antibiotics.

I hadn't heard from Rick at all. That bothered me. I worried that he was angry. Not only had I missed the dance, but his parents had also spent that money on a limo. I had let them all down. Who could blame him if he never spoke to me again? I cared so much about looking good, I had worn myself down.

The same nurse who had given me my IVs came into my room holding another hospital gown. "Put this on backwards so your rump won't show," she said.

"Why do I need to do that? Aren't I going home today? I've got one gown on already."

She left, shutting the door, and although I didn't feel like putting on another gown, I did what she asked. Maybe there was another X ray or test my doctor needed before I could be released.

Suddenly the door swung open and standing before me were my parents holding balloons and a tape player, my two best friends in formals, their dates, and Rick in a tuxedo.

"Would you care for a dance?" Rick asked. "Just because you missed the ROTC dance doesn't mean we can't have our own right here—right now."

Tears came to my eyes. "Sure," I stammered.

The nurse closed the curtains and left only the bathroom light on. My friends coupled together as Rick wrapped his arms around me and began to sway to the music.

"I'm so glad you are okay," he said. "I called your parents every night to check up on you."

"They didn't tell me." I pulled at my hair so it wouldn't look unbrushed.

"Don't worry." He smiled. "You look beautiful."

For what seemed like hours, my friends and I danced. We didn't mind the people watching from the hall or my parents dancing beside us. My two hospital gowns were less than formal, but I didn't care. When the tape was over, Rick helped me into a wheelchair and took me downstairs to the limousine waiting to take me home.

Never will I forget that afternoon for as long as I live. I didn't have my hair fancily done or even a pretty dress, but I learned how to feel truly beautiful—to be loved.

MICHELE WALLACE CAMPANELLI

Mistakes are part of the dues one pays for a full life.
SOPHIA LOREN

TWO STEPS FORWARD, ONE STEP BACK

As I sat *alone on the front steps of our house,* remembering what my friends and I had done just two days ago, I couldn't believe I was part of this horrendous plot. A totally cruel joke was about to play itself out on an innocent and unsuspecting friend.

What had happened to me? Where was that nice person everyone thought I was? Was there some sort of evil spirit lurking deep within me, waiting to attack a mentally challenged girl just to remain in the good graces of my so-called sophisticated friends?

I'd always prided myself on my love of God, family, and friends, on my compassion for those less fortunate than myself. I was a well-rounded teen—a good student, a dancer, and president of our church's Methodist Youth Fellowship. I was the girl voted as having the prettiest smile and figure and the best sense of humor. I was also voted the most Christian! I was the person who helped Audrey, my friend with cerebral palsy, on and off the trolley car and up and down the stairs at school, and shared lunch with her, totally ignoring the comments of those who chose to laugh behind our backs.

Was it only a few days ago that my world was so perfect, that I liked and respected myself and felt confident I was living a life that God would approve of?

I visualized the face of Betty Jane Nelson, the girl who was about to have the disappointment of her young life. I remembered the first time I'd seen her—a tall, large, clumsy girl, who dressed rather plainly. Betty Jane and her family were newcomers to our neighborhood. They had just moved to the big city from a rural community, and by some of my friends' standards, she had "country bumpkin" tattooed on her forehead. But she had a twinkle in her eyes and a smile that could melt even the hardest heart.

Mrs. Nelson, Betty's mom, was the kindest lady I'd ever met. She encouraged our friendship and gave me an open invitation to their home anytime that I wanted to come by. I stopped there several days a week for great homemade cookies and lots of meaningful conversation.

Now, as I contemplated this unfathomable farce, I felt like a traitor. It was a hot summer's day. A group of friends were at my house just sitting around, drinking pop and having a good time. "Since Jerry's not here," Sally said, "why don't we have Bruce call up Betty Jane Nelson and pretend to be Jerry? He could ask her to go to the party with him on Saturday night. You know Jerry's too shy to ask a girl out, so we'll do it for him. Then we'll tell him about it at the last minute, and being the nice guy he is, he'll go through with the date."

I thought it was a rather bad joke to play on Jerry, but wanting to go along with the crowd, remained silent. None of us actually planned to hurt Betty. We all thought the prank would be on Jerry, and she'd have her first real date. Bruce made the call, and an elated Betty said, "Yes!"

Somehow, Jerry found out about the plot the very next day. He called me up and said, "Positively not. I won't do it. Since she's your friend and this little conspiracy took place at your house, you've been chosen to straighten this mess out."

Now, as I sat alone, totally ashamed and sorry for my part in this situation, a Bible verse flashed into my mind, "Now is the accepted time!" I knew what I had to do. I had to go to the Nelsons' home immediately and *fess up*.

I decided to call Betty Jane before going over. When she answered the phone, before I could say anything, she said, "I'm so excited about my date to the party this Saturday night. My mom is making me a new dress. I can hardly wait." The realization of what we'd done became unbearable. Why didn't I speak up when my friends decided to play this terrible joke on Jerry? A silly joke that had backfired and would now hurt Betty instead. I hadn't approved of the joke from the very beginning, but sitting there and saying nothing made me just as responsible as those who had planned the whole plot.

With wobbly legs and a very heavy, repentant heart, I ran the six blocks over to Betty Jane's house. As soon as I walked up the front steps, I started crying uncontrollably. Mrs. Nelson put her arms around me and said, "What's wrong? It can't be all that bad. Come inside and we'll talk about it." As I blurted out the story, I waited for the ax to fall, fully expecting to be escorted right out the front door, banned forever from their home. Quite the opposite happened. Betty Jane said, "That's okay, you're still my friend," and Mrs. Nelson commended me for having the courage to come forward before the whole episode played itself out. We talked a long time about feelings, truths, peer pressure, and going against our morals. When we finished our lengthy conversation, she said, "I've just taken some homemade sweet rolls out of the oven. Let's just forget about the whole thing and start over."

The feeling of total forgiveness was awesome. I was on top of the world again. I knew I had learned a very valuable lesson, a lesson that would stay with me for the rest of my life. A lesson that would mold me into the person I knew I could become, the person God wanted me to be.

RUTH ROCKER

SLEEPING BEAUTY

I n my work as a newspaper columnist, all day long I
listen to the stories of readers who call, suggesting topics for
my column. Some people want to expose injustice; others
want vindication, or a problem solved. It's not often I hear good
news.

But one day I got a call from my friend Susan, a singer whose
husband, Gary, is a choir director at a local high school. Susan
began telling me a story about one of Gary's students, Crystal,
and a little girl named Karly.

Seven-year-old Karly lay in a bed in the intensive care unit at the
local children's hospital in town. It was mid-December, and three
days earlier Karly had had brain surgery. Still she hadn't opened
her eyes or spoken. Her dark hair spread out on a pillow, framing
her pale face. Not awake. Not asleep.

"Karly was in such serious condition," her mother Nancy told
me when I interviewed her. "She'd had such a dangerous surgery. With brain surgery like that, you never know if the person is
going to wind up in a coma or brain-dead. When you can't wake
them up, you just have to wait and hope." Karly had a long list of
medical problems and had endured eleven brain surgeries in her
seven years. She hadn't awakened from this last one.

That December day, Nancy was at Karly's bedside when Gary's
choir came to the ICU to sing holiday songs for the patients.
Nancy heard the music from down the hall. *Karly loves music,* she
thought.

"After we finished one song, a lady came and tapped me on the shoulder," Crystal told me later. Crystal was seventeen and a senior at the high school. "I was standing in the back. She said, 'Would you come with me and sing for a little girl?' So I followed her."

Crystal saw a thin child hooked up to a lot of machines. It looked like she was just sleeping. "From the moment I walked in the room I had a feeling like I was supposed to be there," Crystal said. Ordinarily, Crystal would have refused to sing by herself. She'd been taking voice lessons from my friend Susan for only a few months. "She has a beautiful, rich mezzo-soprano voice," Susan told me. "But Crystal doesn't like to sing solos. She's very shy."

On this day Crystal didn't hesitate. She stood close to the little girl's bed and began to sing "Silent Night." Nurses crowded into the room to watch. Down the hall the other students had finished their last song and headed for the school bus. Crystal didn't care if she was being left behind. She began to sing "Some Children See Him."

"It's a song about children, and she was so little," Crystal says. "I just sang my best and tried to make her feel better. I tried to spin the phrases just for her. I felt like she was trying to hear me."

And then Karly opened her eyes. "She opened them and then she squinted them," Nancy said. "And then she got a big grin on her face. Everyone started crying."

Everyone but Crystal. Crystal was still singing.

When she finished her song, Nancy took a picture of Crystal standing beside Karly's bed. Crystal looked over and saw her choir teacher, Gary, standing in the doorway smiling at her. It was time to go.

In the hours after Crystal left, Karly awakened more completely. It felt like a Christmas miracle to the people who'd seen what happened. But Crystal would never have known the consequence of her song if an amazing coincidence hadn't occurred.

One of ICU the nurses was so touched by what she'd seen, she wrote about it in a Christmas newsletter she tucked into her Christmas cards and mailed to friends a few days later. One of her friends, coincidentally, was a teacher at the same high school where Gary led the choir. She read the story and called Gary.

"We hadn't realized until then that Crystal's song had had that effect," Gary says. Crystal and Gary had not known Karly was in a coma; they had assumed she was just sleeping. My friend Susan called Crystal immediately and told her what she'd done for Karly several days before. "I couldn't believe it, I was so excited," Crystal said later. "I was jumping up and down. I wanted to go sing for her again."

So calls were made, and on Christmas Eve Crystal went back up to the hospital, to Karly's bedside. It was another hard day. "Karly's in a major amount of pain," Nancy told Crystal. "She's been having seizures and has had trouble sleeping." Crystal sat down and sang to Karly for more than an hour. "I sang her to sleep," Crystal says. "I sang her into a peaceful sleep."

Crystal still is amazed at what her singing did that day in December. "It made me realize how powerful music is, and how it changes and affects people.

"It made me realize that music is meant to be in my life." In fact, Crystal decided she would study music therapy in college, and make it her career. Nancy asked that Karly be given music therapy as part of her medical treatments. Her doctor agreed. Musicians began to come to the hospital to play for Karly. Crystal stayed in touch with Karly and her family. She brought Karly gifts. She recorded a tape of songs for Karly. "And when she gets better," Crystal said later that spring, "I'm going to teach her to sing."

MARGIE BOULÉ

SEASONED WITH AGE

*M*y *twelve-year-old-niece, Justine, and her girl-*
friends wanted to help as many sick children at
Christmastime as they could. This year, instead of
just getting clothes, stuffed animals and toys, they wanted to give
to those less fortunate.

Justine and friends decided to give whatever money they had to
buy toys for the kids at their local Ronald McDonald House in
Long Island. They had enthusiasm and time, but they became a
little discouraged when they figured out what they could scrape
together between themselves—hardly enough to buy three Bar-
bies and a box of Legos.

The girls flopped over the old basement furniture Justine's parents had from forever and threw out ideas. One of them came up
with making a flyer on the computer that they could give to kids
at school and neighbors asking them to bring toys and stuffed animals to the house. Justine's mom said she would help them load
the gifts in the van and drive the girls down to Ronald McDonald
House. That felt like a good start.

The girls were taking turns eating popcorn and playing with
the different flyer designs on the computer, searching for just the
perfect one, when one of them spotted a piece of paper wedged in
the side of Justine's great-grandpa's big black leather recliner.

Great-Grandpa didn't live with them. He never had, in fact Justine never knew him, but she knew the story behind the recliner.
Great-Grandpa was ninety when her grandparents bought it for
him, but after two weeks, Great-Grandpa decided he didn't like

the chair and never sat in it again. Her grandparents used the chair for years, then gave it to Justine's uncle, who used it for a while, then gave it to her dad. By the time Justine's family got it, it had been spilled on, chewed on, and cleaned and fixed so many times it was amazing it still worked.

Now here was this piece of paper wedged in solid. They gathered around and tugged until it finally came loose. What they thought was paper was really a tightly folded packet wrapped in the orange-brown butcher paper Justine's great-grandpa used to use at work. There were numbers written on the outside. They thought about opening it themselves, but with the numbers on it, they decided it might be important and took it to my sister-in-law.

"Where'd you find this?" Justine's mom asked.

The girls quickly told her.

"Great-grandpa's chair?" She stared at the numbers written on the outside.

They all gathered around her as she leaned back against the kitchen sink. She turned the packet over in her hands then slid her thumbnail under the yellowed tape. When she folded back the butcher paper, four one-hundred-dollar bills sat in the palm of her hand. They girls squealed and danced around the kitchen teasing Justine's mom and yelling, "Finders keepers!"

As it turned out, Great-Grandpa didn't believe in banks and had been famous for squirreling money away in safe places. It seemed he'd taken the money his son had given him over twenty-five years ago and had hidden it in the recliner. My sister-in-law said it was amazing, with all the moving and shuffling around that chair had been through, that the money hadn't been found before now.

With Great-Grandpa's money and all the donations they collected from family, neighbors, and friends, the girls were able to give as a group in a way they never could have dreamed of given individually. They learned the magic that can happen when they have open and willing hearts. And we all figure Great-Grandpa had something to do with this, and was using his infinite wisdom from on high, just waiting for the perfect way to part with his money. Justine and her friends spent the money wisely, realizing it was seasoned with age.

LORELEI PEPE

III
IF THE SHOE FITS

When I open my mind,
I see more clearly.

JO ANNA BURNS-MILLER

MY MOTHER
THE HELLION

A s a child I always wondered how my mother knew what I was up to. How did she know I had not done my homework, had been smoking (and in my parochial school uniform, too), or had lied about where I had been and with whom? They were such well-constructed and convincing lies. And they had taken me so long to concoct.

Now, looking back, the answer is crystal-clear to me. My mother did not have eyes in the back of her head, nor did she have a needle-sharp sixth sense of perception. The plain, unvarnished truth is . . . my mother was a hellion in her own youth.

My grandmother, rest her soul, was not alive to share this information with me. My grandfather, chief of police in our small town, never incriminated anyone, including his daughter. I simply know this is the answer. How else *could* she know what I was thinking, what I had done, and what I planned to do if she had not already trod the same path herself?

Take, for example, the time our neighbor's canoe was stolen from their yard. Actually, *stolen* is too harsh a word. *Borrowed* is more accurate. With the assistance of my cousin we paddled across the river in the dark to participate in a clandestine meeting of our friends. Because of a slight miscalculation of the tides, we were unable to return until almost daybreak.

The canoe was immediately returned to its rightful owners. Okay, they claimed the side was bashed in. I prefer *dinged*. Stuff happens. My mother said she knew without a doubt I had been involved. I thought she had a lot of crust bandying my name about that way. The perpetrator could have been anyone.

And how about the time she insisted I had been driving her car when she had been away? It certainly was not my fault the gas gauge was down. There could have been a leak. For heaven's sake, I didn't even have my license then. Or the dozens of other peccadilloes she laid at my door, like the cozy little get-togethers at my house when my parents were out. That one always boggled my mind. We were scrupulously careful not to leave any traces, yet I was always found out. Keg parties in the woods, occasional absences from school, fast boys, faster cars, a glorious weekend in New York City (I was supposed to be on a retreat), using false ID and being caught by my—gulp—grandfather.

Okay, I admit there was some truth to that one, but I can explain, honest. Someone once said, "Experience is the best teacher." This is turning out to be true. How else could I know what my own daughter is up to—the little sneak!

ALICIA WILDE HARDING

TO SAVE A LIFE

For so long my friend Daniella has been lying to her family. It's been very difficult making up a life and pretending to be someone she's not. She used to say to herself that she was just acting. But the truth is she's afraid that the moment she tells her mother and grandmother about her real life, they will reject her, maybe never speak to her again.

Lately, she tells me, the questions have been coming too frequently for her to be keeping up the charade. "Are you dating anyone? Any nice boys in Chicago?" her mother would ask during their Sunday phone calls.

After her father's death, Daniella's mother and grandmother are all the family she has. How could she let them down and tell them she's never going to be what they expect? She picked up the phone but quickly hung up. "If they can't accept me for who I am, I'll find someone who will!"

Frustrated, she got in her car and drove around, passing Wrigley Field and the Museum of Science and Industry. Daniella thought about starting over, leaving her family behind. Maybe she could move or change her number to unlisted. She parked in front of a bar, wondering if a drink would make her feel better.

But the moment her foot hit the curb, she saw the animal shelter nearby. "Adopt a Pet," a banner read. Loud barking and raucous squawking filled the air. Daniella decided to go inside and watch a few creatures that might be feeling worse than she was.

As she walked in, her heart melted. Rows and rows of caged cats, dogs, and birds begged for attention, love, and freedom. Tails wagged, cats meowed. What a menagerie! She wished she could adopt each one. All they wanted was to be loved, not rejected.

Suddenly, Daniella realized that these animals had a lot in common with her. They were both just seeking someone to care about them, unconditionally.

"Rocky: quiet, friendly to kids and cats," announced the sign above an interesting-looking Labrador. He had sweet dark eyes and a black shiny coat with tan spots above the eyes, nose, and legs. His tail was wagging wildly with excitement.

Daniella stuck her hand through the door. Instantly, he licked her. The kiss lightened her dark mood. In that moment, she knew Rocky would be a friend who would never judge her!

After Daniella had paid for his shots, the shelter technician led him in. Rocky rocketed over, soaking Daniella's face with kisses until her cheeks were sopping wet. He was happy to have her! She felt completely accepted. The world lifted off her shoulders. No matter what happened with her family, at least Rocky would be a friend who would love her just as she was.

When Daniella got home, she picked up the phone to finally tell her family the truth. Slowly, she stammered to her mother and grandmother, "I am gay." First there was stunned silence at the end of the line. With shocked voices, they told her that they were proud of her for telling them and that they loved her. She felt ecstatic! The conversation continued for nearly an hour. They even asked all about her new pet.

Rocky had given her the courage to tell them the truth. Going to the animal shelter, she thought, was about saving a dog's life. Turns out, Daniella's new pet gave her the courage to save her own.

MICHELE WALLACE CAMPANELLI

You grow up the day you have your
first real laugh—at yourself.
ETHEL BARRYMORE

POETIC JUSTICE

The little nerd said a bright "hello," and I turned my head away so quickly that my ponytail swatted me in the face. I walked faster so he wouldn't think I had paid attention. Better yet, he should know that I had noticed but had purposely ignored him. I wouldn't speak to a boy who was a full year younger, still in fifth grade.

I scanned the street to see if anyone had detected this nonexchange. If it was misunderstood, my name would be intertwined with the twerpy Joshua's on the filthy wall outside the school bathroom, encircled by a red heart and pierced by an arrow.

To my horror, I heard a whistle and looked up to find Eddie on his second-floor balcony. He winked and puffed on a cigarette stuck in the corner of his mouth, James Dean–style. Since he'd grown a fuzz of a mustache—unaccompanied by any other physical changes—the diminutive Eddie had been swaggering and letting out little snickers of superiority. Well, for some of my friends, any attention from an eighth-grader was something to cherish. They'd giggle about it in our sleepovers, huddling under the blankets in the dark. But living across the street from Eddie, our verandas facing each other, I knew him well. I've heard him scream when his father's belt met his bare behind, each whack burning my own. So who did he think he was impressing with that macho act?

With my bad luck, the following week Joshua dared say hello to me again. I mean, I couldn't help but pass him on the street since he lived on my block, but you'd think he'd know his place. Instead, he grinned at me, as if his mother had told him that with those blue eyes he would break the girls' hearts. I decided that I would show him that no matter how many times he showed up as an unexpected sneeze, I had my reputation to uphold. I would never, ever respond.

And I never, ever did. In time, the shrimpy Joshua grew taller and rather broad across the shoulders. I would spot him coming down from two blocks away and brace myself to show him that no matter what, a younger boy was beneath me. As a junior in high school, I wouldn't greet a sophomore and set myself up for ridicule.

He did catch me off guard three years later. He must have enlisted in the navy, because the first time I saw him in white uniform with that cap covering all but wisps of blond hair, I was taken by surprise. And when he gave me that broad-grinned "hello" of his, I almost responded. Luckily, I caught myself in time. I snapped my head and walked away, grateful that my beehive hairdo wouldn't bounce with a life of its own. I did glance up, though, to check whether Eddie had observed me from his perch on the balcony. Thank God he wasn't there. Lately he had been busy at his father's garage, working on his stupid motorcycle that he'd then bring out for a noisy and smoky ride down the street. He seemed so pleased with himself, his laughter would turn into a crooked smirk that looked sexy only on James Dean. I hoped flies got into Eddie's mouth.

After college I did not return to live at home, and anyway, my parents had moved to a more modern section of town. I went on with the business of life: received my law degree and opened my own practice.

It was at a "coming-up-for-air" party that my associate dragged me to after work one evening where I noticed the familiar tall figure. Oh God! The athletic shoulders in the unconstructed linen jacket were topped by chiseled cheeks, with that familiar permanent dimple on the left. His wide face was punctuated by gorgeous blue eyes below thick, light brown hair.

I poked my friend's ribs, jerking my eyes in a gesture for her to take a look at this testosterone-filled specimen.

"What do you know!" she breathed excitedly. "That's Josh. Just made partner at Folsom, Elsworth. Come meet him."

But of course I knew who he was—minus the credentials. Being older and wiser, I was ready to admit that a man who was a year younger could make a good prospect. Especially when he came packaged like this one.

"Joshua," she said, "meet Talia."

"We've met." My sweet smile throbbed with a lifetime of apologies. I extended my hand.

"We have?" he asked, and the familiar smile of the nine-year-old nuisance melted my knees.

"We grew up on the same street," I replied, incredulous.

His dazzling blue eyes went over me with a glance that already contained a dismissal. "I don't remember," he said, his tone bored, and waved to someone above my head. "Enjoy the party." He turned and walked away.

My colleague touched my elbow. "Forget about him. I got this millionaire antiques dealer for you to meet. He got his start fixing up old motorcycles and cars." She pointed to a man slouching against the door, his hair sleeked back James Dean–style. "Come meet Eddie."

TALIA CARNER

BACK-SEAT TRAVELER

"*Make him honk,*" my sister said with a giggle. We looked out the rear window of our parents' 1976 Buick. Traffic rushed around us in a metallic stream of colors.

As part of a military family, we were on the move again, leaving one air force base for another. Up front, Mom and Dad were sipping coffee and deciding which exit to take. Busy navigating, they left us youngsters to play our games.

And this was one of our favorites. I looked at the huge eighteen-wheeler truck behind us, then lifted my arm. Yanking it down a couple times, I caught the driver's eye and smiled. Would he do it?

After a moment's pause, two long blares answered my request, startling the traffic around us. My sister and I cheered, amazed that we had such power. Although we were small, our skinny arms got results. Truck drivers obeyed us.

Over the years, the car trips continued, turning into a family ritual. In back, we draped bedsheets across our windows to block out the sun. Armed with books, snacks and headphones, we tried to block out the ground moving beneath us.

Sometimes, my sister and I fought. Mostly we ignored each other and kept to our sides of the car. As my sister grew older, she developed motion sickness and could not ride in back without feeling sick. The trips became torture for her. The honking game ended and we waited impatiently for our new destinations.

Then my dad retired from the air force and the cross-country trips stopped altogether. But instead of feeling relieved, I felt bereft. I became restless and yearned to be in that back seat once again, miles passing underneath my feet. This "final destination" was turning into a prison, with no chance for escape or new vistas. I wanted out.

Opportunity came during college, when I signed up for a semester in London. At the airport, I stepped on that plane and did not look back. Although I was physically leaving my family, once again I was their little girl riding in the back of a 1976 Buick. I felt safe, happy, cherished, and most of all, hopeful. I was escaping from stability and stepping into something unknown and mysterious. The challenge intrigued me.

But after I unpacked, I discovered my roommates did not exactly share my yearnings. Coming from a military background, I expected everyone to rise early and fit as much sightseeing into a day as possible.

"I'm going to Kew Gardens Sunday morning," I told one of them. "Do you wanna come?"

"What time?"

"Oh, I'll probably get up at eight or so, then leave the house by nine."

My roommate shook her head. "Nah, that's too early. I want to sleep in."

"You sure?"

"Yes, I'm sure. I want to sleep."

Disappointed, I prepared for my solo journey. I packed a small bag with a guidebook, camera, and novel, then set my alarm. Its steady beeping awoke me the next morning, and I got ready for my day, a slight trepidation in my stomach.

In all my years of traveling, I had never been alone. It had always been with my family, and I was always in the back seat. But now I was in the front seat—I was in charge. If I wanted to see Kew Gardens, I had to do it alone. No one else would get up this early on a Sunday morning.

I slipped out of the flat and walked down to the tube. Arriving at the train station, I purchased a ticket and stood on the platform. I was scared. London was one of the biggest cities in the world, and it was just me—no roommates, no family. I looked at the people around me suspiciously. What if they tried to harm me? What would I do?

I gathered my bag closer to my side and waited. The train arrived and I took my seat. My heart was pounding. Only a few people sat nearby, lost in their own world. They stared out the window or read a newspaper and waited for the train to depart. It did, with a lurch, and we were off.

I put on my headphones and listened to some country music, trying to relax. But I was tense. What if I was going in the wrong direction? What if I missed my stop?

The train began to rock, and leaning back in my seat, I let the motion calm me. At each new stop, I studied the people getting on and off the train—some by themselves, others in pairs, all of them strangers. But I was not afraid. The morning air was cool and misty each time the doors opened. And through my train window, I could see old brick buildings and rolling green fields. They blurred together in peaceful harmony underneath the cloudy sky, the softest pastel hues.

When my station arrived, I stepped off the train, and since I did not know where to go, I followed some strangers who were headed to the gardens. With each step, I gained more confidence. I was going in the right direction. I was safe. I trusted my surroundings. And more important, I trusted myself.

I spent nearly the whole day at Kew Gardens, alone. And somehow the solitude made it more meaningful. I took in the roses, the quiet fields, and the call of birds without having to consider another person's needs or desires. Unconstrained, I was free to explore and think with only nature filling my eyes and ears.

That semester, there would be more solo trips, as sleepy roommates rolled over and refused to get up before noon. But I discovered that being alone and depending on myself was one of the most important things I would learn. With each trip, I became more aware of my strengths and weaknesses as an individual. Yes, I got lost, but the fear and self-doubt were gone. I was free to concentrate on the beauty of my surroundings and the pleasure of travel.

The little girl was still inside me, excited about the prospect of seeing something new and foreign. But instead of pulling an imaginary horn to feel powerful, she discovered that self-reliance and choice resulted in real power. And instead of being in the back seat, she was now up in front, manning the wheel, controlling the direction her life would take.

KATHLEEN STURGEON

JOLLY GREEN GIANT

"*H*ey Jolly!*"
"Look, it's the Jolly Green Giant!"
"In the Valley of the Jolly, ho-ho-ho, Green Giant,"
they sang.

Taunting. Teasing. The words slipped out of pretty-complexioned, no-braces-on-perfect-teeth, bouncing-ponytailed girls. Cassidy grade school classmates. A light drizzling rain slid off my hand-me-down black and yellow slicker. I tried to grow small, believing that if I was lucky, I might disappear.

Giggles spun out over the warm spring air. Light, innocent giggles bubbled into whispers. The words "Jolly Green Giant" slipped with casual indifference from their glossy pink lips. I saw myself as the lumbering Giant stuck on a larger-than-life can of green peas, just like in the advertisement. Stuck with that nickname and image—glued into the minds of the "cool, popular girls" as a jolly, oversized geek.

I remember laughing. Smiling. Freezing. Speaking with another voice—painfully self-conscious of my height (at five foot five, I had my adult height in the sixth grade) and of my dishwater bangs hiding a not so peaches-and-cream complexion.

Standing outside Wheeler's Drugstore on that particular May afternoon in the late sixties, I felt like the ugly duckling of the Cassidy sixth-grade class. As if all the girls in the sixth grade were getting ready for a prom to which I had somehow managed not to be invited. A teenage girl—still a child, really—grown tall and awkward before her time. Blinking back tears, I watched the cool girls walk away in their matching sweaters and skirts. Then, slowly, when I was sure it was safe, I picked up my cello and walked home.

And the "cool" girls, in time, walked out of my life. As I look back, they were not mean-spirited, just ignorant of the child they wounded with a silly nickname, unaware that my parents had ruined my life by moving me across town to a new neighborhood that past summer. For the first three months, I ate alone in the orchestra room. Eating Swiss cheese on club crackers and practicing "The Swan" (a cello solo) became my daily lunchtime ritual. Of course, there were several family attempts to rescue me. My Border Collie, Bonnie, walked with me to school and stayed till the bell rang, and my dad occasionally picked me up and whisked me off for a soda and thirty minutes of dad-daughter pep talk.

After the black and yellow rain slicker incident, however, I decided to confide my secret to my grandfather, who lived with my family. At eighty-five, he spent a great deal of time in his garden or at his desk, ordering smelly cheeses from Monk's and bulbs from distant lands and reading the Bible.

"Grandfather?" I knocked on his door.

"Hello, Granddaughter Number Two. Come in."

He was sitting in his rocking chair, listening to a Rachmaninoff piano concerto. As I stepped into the muted light, I caught my breath—the room smelled of sweet pipe tobacco and dark, rich chocolate. He broke off a piece of the Blue Monday chocolate, and I confided about the nickname and the ponytail girls. He listened. Then, curiously, he folded a paper, saved a caterpillar crawling up his arm, and opened the door. It was a small gesture, one of simple kindness. "When God looks at a caterpillar, He sees the butterfly." Then he unwrapped a second Blue Monday, offered the whole candy palm-flat. "After college," he said, "I moved to Louisville, where I didn't know anyone. I went to church and there was this young lady in a funny-looking hat. I took a chance, sat down, and introduced myself. Her name was Maude." He licked the chocolate off his fingers. "That was your grandmother." He paused. "Open your eyes, Granddaughter. Open your eyes."

The next day at school, the bell rang for lunch. I started to go to the orchestra room but changed by mind. Instead, fighting the urge to run away, I entered the cafeteria. A sea of students wafted before me. I got my tray and walked through the line. "Please . . ." I prayed to the cafeteria gods. Please what? I wasn't sure. Then I saw her. Sitting alone at a table by the window, with cropped, curly brown hair, her head bent over her lunch box.

"Hello," I said.

She looked up, surprised and delighted. "Hi."

"Is anyone sitting here?"

"No." Her face lit up. She had a pretty face—and the look of a child out of a fairy tale. As I pulled out my chair, I saw the violin.

"You play?"

"Yes."

"Oh, I play the cello."

"Really? Do you know Saint-Saëns' 'The Swan'?"

In time, the girl sitting alone in the cafeteria became my best friend. Through middle school and high school, we studied together. Made the same grades and missed the same questions on tests. We played in Youth Orchestra and dreamed of going off to the same college. After graduation, my friend's father accepted a teaching position in Australia. I went to college, where she joined me in my sophomore year. We were roommates and sorority sisters at Northwestern, and later entered law school together. And now we are "ducklings" who grew up to be lawyers. I don't think either of us still plays the violin or the cello, but she has a little boy, and I have three little girls. Just yesterday, over a supper of tuna and noodles, my oldest daughter, Meredith, confided, "No one likes me. I'm a dork. There's no one for me to sit with at lunch."

"Really? How about if I come for lunch tomorrow?"

As I walked across the Cassidy school playground, giggles floated out over the same sizzling hot asphalt where I once played four-square. Ponytails bounced wildly. Some things do not change. I walked down the same long hallway, where different drawings of butterflies and dinosaurs decorated the same white-washed walls. Near the gym, I hesitated, glanced through the open doors, and remembered the tall, shy child called Jolly.

A voice called me back to the present moment. From a long line of children, a little blond-haired girl smiled at me. It was Meredith, the smallest girl in her class, maybe in the school. (Life has a curious way of playing tricks; turning tall into small and caterpillars into memories.) We walked through the cafeteria line. Then, as we turned, I saw anxiety cloud her eyes. "There's no place to sit," she whispered.

"Why sure there is." We carried our trays to an empty table and as we dipped French fries into ketchup, I glanced around the cafeteria. Near the window, there was another little girl. Sitting alone. She had long braids tied up with plaid ribbons.

"Meredith, who is . . ."

Following my gaze, my daughter answered, "Her name's Anna. She moved here from South Africa."

"Oh really?"

Then, curiously, we both saw—at the exact same instant—a banner hanging over the window near Anna's table. A slight breeze blew the brightly colored strip of cloth, back and forth, creating the impression of a graceful giant Monarch butterfly suspended in flight. We both read the words, painted in sunflower yellow and brilliant blue, "IF IT'S GOING TO BE, IT'S UP TO ME."

Meredith smiled, got up, and walked over to Anna's table.

"Hi. Is anyone sitting here?"

Anna looked up, smiling. Braces, blue and pink, caught the light. "Oh, hello." She beamed.

As Anna pulled out a chair for Meredith, she carefully placed something on the floor. I glanced beneath the table and saw a violin.

MARGARET C. PRICE

Revenge may not be a particularly higher
consciousness-oriented activity.
CARRIE FISHER

HOT CHOCOLATE
AND REVENGE

*T*he day began with such promise. Far away from the rigors of college life and my apple-green dorm room, sun peeked through puffy white clouds and glinted on snow-frosted trees as my three dear and trusted girlfriends—Debbie, Kerry, and Chris—and I arrived at Hoo Doo Ski Bowl on the slopes of Mt. Hood in the Pacific Northwest. Anticipation of my first downhill skiing experience left me fidgeting with excitement and nervousness.

I watched as others easily slid up the bunny hill, assisted by the rope tow. *This is going to be a snap!* I thought, buoyant with newfound confidence. Grabbing tightly onto the rope instead of letting it glide through my grasp, I moved a few inches . . . and quickly fell flat on my face. Struggling to my feet, I took the rope a second time—and fell again. And again. And *again!*

The sixth time I went down, I just stayed there, sprawled, too tired and embarrassed to move. A little boy of about eight skied over to where I lay. Looking down at me sympathetically, he said, "Lady, do you need help up?" *Up, that sounds like a nice direction,* I thought. "Yeah, I think I do," I replied more humbly. I was eighteen years old and getting more ancient by the minute!

After pulling me to my feet, the kid began skiing away with no effort. Looking back over his shoulder—while he still skied—he tossed me some hope, "I know you'll do okay, lady. This is my first time, too." I hated that kid.

Finally making it to the top of the bunny hill, I triumphantly and unexpectedly glided down the almost flat slope in a smooth, ever-so-straight line. My friends, thinking I had reached a certain level of adeptness, talked me into going up in the chair lift. Of course I trusted them.

After a lot of frustration and a little help from a ski instructor (at least he was older than eight), I sidestepped up the steep ramp to the lift. When the next double chair swung around the pole, I plopped down next to Chris. Debbie and Kerry rode "backup."

Surrounded once again by my friends, I regained my composure as away we soared high above the treetops and crisp, white snow. This was why I had come, I understood, as I found myself caught in a white winter dream. Sheer beauty, until we neared the end of the ride, and what was that—small pellets? Small pellets of ice, pelting our faces!

What will this mean? the beginner in me wondered, but there was no time to form an answer. As I scooted off the chair lift, my skis immediately hit a solid crust of ice the moment they touched ground. With nary a chance to alter fate, Chris and I dove head-first down the ramp's steep incline, landing in a pick-up-sticks tangle of arms and legs, skis and poles. Like troops to the rescue, Debbie and Kerry came up behind us, laughing hysterically.

"We wondered what happened to you guys! You were there, and then you weren't," they sputtered, eventually helping us, in between more fits of laughter, to disconnect our knotted limbs.

Then, before I could barely stand on my own, my legs feeling as wobbly as Bambi's, my so-called friends abandoned me! With only a word and not even a prayer, they counseled me to lean into the slope and keep my weight on my downhill ski. Yeah, right. Looking down the steep slope, I suddenly realized where they had gotten the name for the ski bowl: Hoo Doo, as in *"Who do you think you are, even trying something like this?"*

With a wall of snow on my right, and an abrupt, death-defying cliff on my left, I began my miserable descent. Unable to zigzag, I made it up as I went: ski to one side, fall, get up, ski to the other side, fall, get up. Back and forth, and back and forth, determined to reach the bottom of the hill, even if it killed me, which it seemed to promise at every turn! Where was that little boy when I needed him?

The only things that drove me on were images of hot chocolate and thoughts of revenge. Certainly not the other skiers whizzing by hollering, "Get outta the way. Get outta the way!" And my girl-friends? Nowhere to be found! *Just wait,* I thought as I stubbornly clenched my jaw. White-knuckled under my gray woolen mittens, I resolutely continued on, determined beyond measure to conquer this snowy demon, knowing it would surely take forever.

But just as suddenly as my agony had begun, my ordeal ended, as if the snow gods had taken pity on me. I miraculously stood at the bottom of the long, icy, wicked white hill, looking up toward the top, wondering how I had even made it down. At certain moments in your life, you define success simply. If you're still standing, that's it.

I pondered all of this, remembering vividly how humiliated and vulnerable I felt standing alone at the top of that steep slope. As I sipped hot chocolate in the ski lodge, I plotted dozens of ways to get revenge on my friends.

Let's see . . . a month of my friends rising at dawn to attend my 7:00 A.M. Prehistoric Anthropology class, tortuously taking notes for me by hand, all without any coffee. While I sleep in, of course! Ah-h, that sounds so good, even my feet are getting warm.

No, scratch that. Too easy for them and not a bit humiliating. How about they'd have to walk all week long around campus in their boots and skis. Maybe then they'd understand just how deadly those things really are and how silly I felt!

Oh wait, wait. I know. They should all have to pose as nude models for the Life Drawing class. Yeah, let them see what it feels like to be exposed and vulnerable to the elements, with everyone staring at them and thinking, *Oh those poor idiots. Don't they know what they're doing?* "It'll be a snap," I'd tell them confidently. And then, while they're posing nervously in front of all those inquiring eyes, I'd walk up and comfortingly reach out to them. "Here you go, girlfriends, you might need this." A steaming mug of hot chocolate.

Nothing like a little sweet revenge.

LISA ROBERTSON

THE BIG SECRET

veryone knew what it was, but they weren't telling me. I carried that vague feeling around all through my childhood. The secret was always one room away where the grown-ups sat and talked, or it was hidden behind hands shielding mouths that whispered and spelled. The more the secret was kept from me, the bigger it got.

I wondered when my day of enlightenment would come. Would it be at the end of my childhood, the day I became a teenager? When that day arrived, nothing happened. I still looked like the twelve-year-old I was the day before, and worse yet, I still acted like a twelve-year-old. And no one had told me a thing about sex.

I was told children came from cabbage patches or from swallowing a watermelon seed. Women in the family way had a bun in the oven. Needless to say, I thought it had something to do with food. I was further diverted from the truth when my teachers talked about birds and bees and pollination. The subtleties of what they were saying never reached me.

Becoming an adult and finding out the big secret was something that was on my mind a lot. To me, an adult was someone who drank coffee, had long, boring conversations, and knew the big secret.

As far as boys went, I thought most of them were callous and cruel, but I couldn't help adoring selected ones at school and teen idols from magazines. These were silent, agonizing, one-sided affairs.

My own physical development, albeit a very slow process, eventually led to feelings of mortification when my older sister proclaimed, in front of the whole family at the dinner table, that it was about time Mother bought me a bra. It was for the best, really, that I didn't know that announcement was just a forerunner to what still ranks as the single most embarrassing moment in my life.

That very week, my mother dragged me, her most painfully modest daughter, to the town's only department store. Because she didn't want to miss the bus back home, she and the saleslady tried the bra on over my clothes in front of everyone walking through the store. The only thing that could have made it worse would have been to stand me in the window on Main Street. Maybe I didn't really want to be a grown-up and know any more about the big secret.

Listening to the jokes circulating in junior high school only added confusion to figuring out the big secret. I laughed with the others, but I didn't really understand what they were talking about. It was only a matter of time before I got caught laughing in the wrong places.

I was halfway through the decade of sexual revolution and free love, but all of that seemed to be happening in a parallel dimension and to other people.

One day, in a stroke of genius, I went to the dictionary at school. Placed on a pedestal in the library, the book was enormous and always opened to the center. I leafed to the S's. Not only was "sex" listed, but other sex-related words were as well. *A gold mine,* I thought. The big secret would finally be revealed to me! A look to the left, then to the right. No one was watching.

"Sex," the book said, was "intercourse." That didn't help. Go on to the next one.

"Sexual" was "relating to, involving, or characteristic of sex, sexuality or the sexes." Still too vague. There were three more. One had to be it!

But sexagenarian, sexennial, and sextuplet, disappointingly, all had to do with the number six.

I paused and slumped over the pedestal, only to rear up with *Quick! Turn to intercourse!*

"Where two roads meet." What happened to the sex?

I decided two things after that day. First, Daniel Webster probably didn't have any descendants, and second, there had to be a national conspiracy helping our parents keep the secret from us. The conspiracy was probably headed up by the same people who kept us from seeing Elvis below the waist.

Unexpectedly, I found plenty of sex in church. That was where the sinners went, after all. People were "begetting" all through the Old Testament. The Song of Solomon was all about love, beautiful but woefully just five little pages. Abraham had lain with his wife's handmaiden. A piece of the secret revealed; you had to be horizontal. Now we're getting somewhere!

I don't know the exact date my childhood was officially over, but I did become an adult. I learned to make adult conversation and to eventually drink coffee. As for the big secret, well, I learned it in spite of my parents' silence on the subject, in spite of my schoolmates, and in spite of the national conspiracy. It was a journey of discovery my husband and I took together, which was what I suspect my parents were trying to accomplish all along. Now, when I look back on it, learning those things gradually, over a period of time, with my life mate, was the most romantic time of my life. And I wouldn't trade that for anything.

LINDA L.S. KNOUSE

It's not what you're eating, it's what's eating you?
JANET GREESON

STARVING

When I was sixteen, I stopped eating. I am a stubborn person by nature, so once I realized I had grown into the next dress size, I just stopped putting food on the fork. Diets and exercise programs didn't do it for a girl who wanted to lose the weight right now. Starving myself seemed the only real option.

I picked at the smallest portions of food Mom would let me get away with, shedding fifty-five pounds over six months. I dropped to ninety-nine pounds.

For a year I maintained that weight. All I could see when I looked in the mirror was all the bodies and faces sexier and prettier than mine. I was so obsessed with looking good that I couldn't see my rib cage and collarbone protruding. All I saw was a girl who wasn't perfect, who wasn't the best she could be.

At first I ignored all the warning signs that I could be that "A" word. I would wake up in the middle of the night as my muscles cramped and convulsed. My insides were withering up and dying, but I ignored the pain.

I convinced myself that too much exercise or growing pains were to blame. When I stopped menstruating I chalked it up to stress. After a whole year of my not having my period, Mom took me to see a doctor.

The physician did an internal exam and tested numerous vials of blood for every disease under the sun. She saw how skinny I was but didn't ask Mom or me a single question about my eating habits. Perhaps, because I was seeing this doctor for the first time, she felt uncomfortable asking, but in the end, I was happy with her proclamation of my good health. I strolled out of the doctor's office unquestioned and free while Mom walked out with her critical question unanswered, "What's wrong with my daughter?"

Realizing there was a serious problem, my parents tried to address it in their own unique ways. Dad yelled at me, screamed at me to "Stop this nonsense and start eating!" Mom, on the other hand, sneaked extra fattening treats onto my plate and into my lunch box to entice me to eat. They both tried to help me, but what do you do when your daughter won't eat?

Nobody knew how to approach me or talk about my weight loss. I disagreed with my concerned family that there was need to worry, because I truly believed nothing was wrong with me.

At the end of my senior year in high school, at eighty-eight pounds, I was scheduled to run the 800- and 200-meter races as a final exam for my PE class. I had prepared myself with practice attempts, sprint sessions, and stretching.

By the second lap of the 800 run, I felt as if I was at the tail end of a major marathon. My legs and arms felt twenty times heavier than they were, my throat was on fire, my head spun, and my vision blurred.

My older sister, Kylie, had come that day to support me. When she saw me struggling, she ran to my side and encouraged me to speed up and keep going. But I just couldn't do it. My mind screamed, "Push on!" while my body cried, "No!" Suddenly, I stopped, wavered, then collapsed into my sister's arms in frustration and embarrassment, ashamed and humiliated by what my classmates and teacher might think.

Even though school was still in session, my sister took me by the shoulders and led me to the car. She held me, listening to me holler and cry until I was red and puffy. She knew I had to come to the realization of how sick I was, and in her infinite beauty, she held and comforted me while I acknowledged that I needed help.

Looking back at photos of myself, I cringe at the shriveled stranger staring back. I thought I had control over my life, when I really had no idea of how out of control I was.

A couple of weeks ago, my whole experience with anorexia came full circle when my minister gave a sermon on the importance of loving yourself. He quoted from the good book: "Love thy neighbor as thyself." He explained that only in taking care of yourself could you become fit to help others. I fought back tears. Even though I am over the physical part of my disease, I had never gained an emotional or spiritual understanding of what had happened. I realized for the first time how incredibly selfish and vain I had been, how my obsession with the way I looked touched those closest to me. Back then, I couldn't see the effect I had on family and friends, and because I didn't take care of myself, I had nothing to give.

I am now a healthy 154 pounds. I may not have washboard abs or sculpted thighs, but I have an inner strength independent of my mirror's reflection. The gift in learning to love myself has been in discovering how far-reaching love can be; how the gentler I am with myself, the more open and compassionate I am with others. They in turn reflect that love, feeding a place in me beyond mirrors or magazine glossies of wafer-thin bodies. Fashioning a life in love never goes out of style.

MICHELLE DUNN

Yaaaaaawn! *I awoke late on Sunday morning with droopy eyes.* I had not nearly caught up on all the sleep I had lost in the past few nights. In the comfort of my room, I secretly wished I could go back to sleep. The warm covers on the wide, downy bed seemed to lull me back into dreamland, but as my mind willed itself back to sleep, my body jumped out of bed. Sleepily, I walked to the shower, wondering why I had ever gotten involved with this sleep-depriving, Sunday-bashing, memory-testing play. Ah yes, I remember. I seem to recall a newspaper clip. . . .

It was a sunny day of my eleventh year when I received the newspaper announcement. A friend of mine who was involved in large theatrical productions had referred me to a professional theater group nearby where a musical, *The Music Man,* would take place. I was really excited. Although I was familiar with the theater, I still had not been involved in any large productions. The thought of being in one exhilarated me. After reading, analyzing, and dreaming about the clip, I was led to go to the casting call.

Although many of the days that followed are blank in my mind, the night of the tryouts will always be firmly planted in there.

My mother hugged me tight and said, "I'm so proud of you. I never would have done this. You have great courage, Carolyn."

Then my father and I hopped into the car and drove into the starry night, past the neighborhood where we lived, farther than the glades of trees in the distance, to a park in the woods. We drove up to the building lit with twinkling lights. Shivering, my father and I ran out of the car into the shadowy umbra. Then we swung open the door and ran into the bright, crowded room.

The hum of the crowd talking almost drowned out the voice of the pleasant secretary. She handed me a form of questions and said, "You are number 64. Please fill out this form, and when you are finished, return it and enter the theater." She vaguely pointed to the open doors on either side of the lobby. My father and I walked across the tiles to a nearby corner, where I proceeded to complete the application.

Most of the questions were fairly easy to answer, such as, "What is your name?" or, "Would you be willing to work on the stage crew?" So when I read the question, "What days would you be unable to come to practice?" it took a surprising amount of thought.

"Dad," I asked quietly, "what days are filled on my schedule?"

"Sundays," he answered automatically, as it was our religion not to participate in outside activities on the Sabbath.

That, I scribbled on the long line following the question. A crick was beginning to form in the back of my neck as I finished the form. I stretched, turned the form in, and entered the theater. I was immediately swept off my feet. Just a few steps into the house, I could hear the voices of talented actors and actresses singing their hearts out on the cluttered stage that had not yet been cleaned from the last performance. The curtains, chairs, and even leftover programs seemed to make this audition even more real. With my father, I sat down on a red padded chair to wait my turn.

As the night crept on, I finally heard my number, 64, and walked onto the stage, just now beginning to doubt myself. I sang a cute little song that I had learned and my mother had helped me to choreograph. Afterward, I was ushered back to learn the dance. Stumbling around the equipment on stage, I tried desperately to elaborate on my limited footwork.

Then I waited nervously to hear my number in the list of callbacks. "12, 29, 30, 44, 51, 56, 64, 89 . . . ," the voice of the short, stocky director called vigorously from the center of the stage. It was all I could do to keep from leaping with joy.

Driving home with my father, I slept nearly the whole way. I could hardly wait to see what the audition would bring.

No one can truly explain how I received the part, I just did. Sometimes I wonder if it was more or less because I was a pianist, as it was required of my part. But whatever the reason, I found myself playing the role of Amaryllis at the first practice. The kindly lady passing out schedules hardly knew how much frustration they would bring me. Listed in red were the sixteen performances for each week in May, four on Sundays.

I was furious! How could the directors have put me in the position of having to choose between church and my true love, acting? I was already fascinated by the play and yearned for my copy of the script. I could hardly wait to memorize my lines or sing with the townspeople. My heart cried out, *You deserve to stay in the play. You are Amaryllis. Are you going to throw it all away?*

I wanted to stay in the play, and I crumpled under the temptation. I made no move to quit. I grew to love my character, the people, and the directors. I loved the costumes, the scripts, the dress rehearsals, and the makeup. I became a star.

Slowly, I trudged to the shower on the last Sunday performance. By now I knew the choice I had made was wrong. Once again, instead of going to church and enjoying the holy day of rest, I would sing my heart out on a stage in front of people I didn't know. That's when I heard that still, small voice say, "It's okay, dear one. You will never do it again."

Now, two years later, at thirteen, I'm being tested again.

"Just ask him," one of the girls said. "If you like a guy, you should ask him out!"

She was referring to my latest crush. At her statement, all the girls nodded in agreement, then looked to me for a reply.

It seemed so harmless. I could even picture us together, holding hands and walking down the sidewalks of our outdoor campus.

"I can't," I explained. "In my church, we believe that God does not want us to date until age sixteen."

Suddenly the bittersweet memory of the play and the choice I'd made not so many years ago came into focus to remind me of how far I'd come. I remembered my turmoil for going against what I believe in. I smiled, feeling self-assured.

By having boundaries in my faith to guide me, I'm free from guilt and free from remorse. Ironically, those very lines in the sand—lines that some may see as confining—have given me all the happiness and freedom I need.

CAROLYN BERG

IV
DOING MY OWN DANCE

You are the story teller of your own life, and

you can create your own legend or not.

ISABEL ALLENDE

"**K**irsten Snyder from Lane County Ice," the announcer called.

"Good luck," said my coach, Cindy, as she squeezed my hand.

I heard the crowd clapping and cheering as I stepped on the ice. My skating friends shouted, "Go, Kirsten!" I tried hard not to blush, but a grin crept over my face just like it always did whenever my friends called out their support to me. I reached my starting spot on the ice and took my opening position. I hoped all the hard work and many hours of practice would help me achieve my dream to win.

My music began—a selection from the motion picture soundtrack of *Patch Adams*. Like a light stroke of a paintbrush on a canvas, my arm drew across my body, and my eyes followed out to my fingertips. I pushed off on my left foot with three powerful strokes into a Mohawk followed by a loop jump. I smiled as my blade curved a clean cut through the ice, and I held the landing, making sure all the judges could see. I pumped my legs with powerful crossovers until I was at the corner of the rink. I stretched my leg and jabbed my toe pick into the ice, which lifted me into a flip jump. *Yes!* I thought and gave another giant smile.

My next moves needed to match the beats of the music exactly. I did a waltz jump, with a ballet jump following. I could hear the music; I was going too fast. I did some fancy three turns so that the music would catch up. Now! *Tinkle, tinkle, tinkle.* I danced on my toes to the high notes of the piano. I tightened my body for my low, fast sit spin and came out of the spin with two back crossovers. So far, things were going great. My energy was high as I followed the music in my mind.

Already it was time to wind up my program. My last 45 seconds included required footwork, a combination jump, and a sequence of spirals. To position myself for my footwork, I prepared to do a second Mohawk. I swayed my leg. Then suddenly my foot slipped out from underneath me, and I hit the ice with a thud. The crowd gasped. My teeth were jarred from the impact, but I popped right back up.

I had never fallen in a competition before, and my first thought was to skate off the ice into my parents' comforting arms. I had worked so hard, and now I felt like I had thrown it all away. After all the hours I had spent preparing, why did I have to fall on such a simple maneuver in front of an audience? The judges would never award me a first. I had ruined everything.

But in that same instant, I kept going. I remembered my coach saying, "The skater who gets up and keeps going, no matter how hard it is, is truly a winner." I remembered my parents telling me, "It doesn't matter whether you come in first or last as long as you try your hardest and enjoy yourself." I had worked too hard to quit now. I was determined to focus.

I smiled as I skated toward my flip-loop combination and landed with a wobble. The crowd clapped enthusiastically and my music began to slow to the end. I stretched my back leg for a spiral sequence across the ice. I stretched from one edge to another, lowered my leg, and did a slow back pivot to a standing pose with my chest in the air and my head and arms arched back. The crowd applauded loudly as I bowed and skated off the ice.

I stopped at the boards and stepped of the ice. Cindy smiled encouragingly, and my parents hugged me tight, whispering in my ear that I had done a wonderful job. I slipped on my guards and sat down on the bench. I was still breathing hard and my legs wouldn't stop shaking. As I waited for my score to be posted, I thought about how much I love this sport, and I decided it didn't matter what I had placed.

Later that evening I was scheduled to skate a pairs performance with my friend Anna, so my parents and I decided to go back to the motel to rest. I changed into some warm-ups, smoothed my purple velvet ice dress, and tucked it into my skating bag. As we walked out of the ice rink toward our car, Courtney, one of my skating friends, asked what I had placed.

"I won third place," I told her proudly.

"That's great, Kirsten," she said. "And good luck tonight."

"Thanks, Courtney." I replied.

As we drove back to the motel, I thought about my day. I had grown up a lot, and I had a new way of looking at performing. I truly realized what my coach, Cindy, meant when she said, "When you fall, especially in a performance, you get stronger, because when you finish something, even if it's not perfect, there is a feeling of accomplishment." I was a winner today because I got up and finished my routine with a smile.

When I am skating, I feel relaxed, peaceful, and as light as the sand crystals that blow along the beach. What matters is that every day I am learning and trying my best. What matters is that I love to skate.

KIRSTEN SNYDER

I finally figured out the only reason to be alive is to enjoy it.
RITA MAE BROWN

WINDOWS OF OPPORTUNITY

*There are moments when I close my eyes and visu-
alize Earth from the black, star-sprinkled atmosphere
of outer space.* I zoom into the greens and blues of the
planet and pick a new corner to explore. It is these dreams of journeys, exploration, and discovery that have taken me from my
teens to my early twenties.

When I was growing up, my wanderlust centered on traveling
the United States. When I was a college sophomore, a good friend
convinced me to study a semester in Seville, Spain. So many new
doors opened! I went from poking around my own backyard to
discovering another culture.

My appetite whetted, I took a postgraduation trip in May 1998
through Australia, New Zealand, and Fiji. I met loads of travelers
on year long sojourns and thought, *I need to do this!*

After returning home, I worked for a year, carefully budgeting
every penny, sacrificing nights out with friends, new clothes, and
living in a place of my own. I stayed on with my parents (who were
gracious enough to let me!) and organized the trip on my own. I decided on destinations, chose the dates, then researched and scheduled flights, rail trips, and lodging. The consummate moment
would be ringing in the new millennium in Sydney, Australia.

In the fall of 1999, I embarked on my dream trip—two months with my best friend and five months on my own exploring Asia and the South Pacific. My journey proved to be a time of deep exploration, not only of different cultures, natural wonders, and extreme climates, but also of my own limitations and curiosities as a stranger in a strange land.

Vietnam opened into emerald green rice fields, the dizziness of crowded marketplaces, an ocean of cone-shaped bamboo hats, and the constant churning of bicycles. Bumpy bus trips gave me time to gaze out the window and absorb my surroundings. I remember one stretch of road in particular—tattered homes on stilts bordered our winding road as dusk began to settle in. I caught glimpses of the people in these homes. The dim gray glow of televisions reflected families in silhouette. As I peered through the bus window into those tiny homes, I saw my own family in Minneapolis and rejoiced in memories of their friendship and love. I developed a real appreciation for these people who were different in so many ways, yet clearly the same.

In Nepal, Manang was our first rest stop along a 220-mile trek through the Nepalese Himalayas. We had two days to explore the glaciers, trails, river, cliffs, and snowcapped peaks. Seated on a ledge, I took a deep breath, inhaling my spectacular surroundings. Below me a blue-gold river flowed smoothly, as birds wind-surfed air currents over patches of bright green pines. It seemed as if time stood still for a few precious heartbeats. Here I was, living my dream on the roof of the world.

By the time I made it to Sydney, my friend had headed for home, but other friends and family had joined me, as well as a million other people, in ushering in the new millennium. Partygoers in my group danced as music poured from huge speakers. The harbor was at its best, lit by boatloads of revelers and the glow of surrounding buildings. People congregated on the shore ringing the harbor. They waved champagne bottles and light sticks, beat drums, cranked noisemakers, tooted horns, and popped confetti-filled Christmas crackers. I stood there for a moment over-whelmed by the spectacle. My mind skipped to the countless hours I'd spent daydreaming about this very moment. As I tried to breathe in my surroundings, to somehow seal this instant inside myself, my family began to count down the final seconds of the twentieth century. Five-four-three-two-ONE!

The sky flooded as a barrage of fireworks was catapulted from the Sydney Harbor Bridge. The water offered up a reflection of sound and light as each new display pelted up over the city and sparkled down toward the water and the merrymakers below. Skyscrapers sent streaks of multihued pyrotechnics off in every direction.

Hugs, kisses, screams, and cheers were still in great abundance as the final fireworks launched us into the fresh century. The air slowly cleared of the colored fog the celebration had created, and music filled the void left by the end of the fireworks show.

We continued our revelry well into the morning, dancing, cele-brating, and living this moment to the limit. For one night, every country in the world had stopped to mark the moment. People across the globe had put aside their differences and come together in celebration of this landmark event.

As we left our millennium party, I gazed up to the Sydney Har-bor Bridge one last time. The word ETERNITY stretched out across the dawn of the new century in bold electric white letters. I thought about my journey and how each place carved a piece of itself into me. I had made my dream come true.

Part of my soul's purpose had been defined, and I had been lucky enough to recognize my wanderlust as valid and to act upon it. My spiritual compass had led me in my travels, and by my light-ness of heart I could tell I had touched "true north."

KATIE SNYDER

*Y*ou know, it's funny the way things seem to happen. Five minutes of one day can change the rest of your life. I know it did mine. And that change taught me that letting loose and giving in to a spur-of-the-moment idea is what life is all about.

I recently was given the opportunity to do research on fruit flies through an eight-week summer program for high school students funded by NASA at Cornell University. I headed out from Florida to the college town of Ithaca, New York, alone and free, not knowing what adventures lay before me.

One weekend, my friends and I were fighting boredom, staring blindly out the window. It was clear we needed to get out and do something, anything. So we headed for the mall. We wandered around the commercial paradise in search of enlightenment, or simply something to do. I discovered our afternoon diversion in a small-sized bottle of blue hair spray. "Let's color our hair blue!" I said spontaneously.

We received a few strange glances on the bus ride back to campus, but most of the occupants were either too old or too tired to notice a bunch of crazy kids, and I admit I was a little disappointed at their indifference. After all, our hair was blue!

Later, when we went out for dinner, we got an entirely different reaction. We were waiting for another friend to meet us in front of a beautiful gray stone church not far from our dorms. For the first time, I felt extremely nervous about how others would react to my appearance. I worried about being on campus in broad daylight with blue hair, but all three of us idiots quickly reminded ourselves that we weren't going to see anyone who knew us anyway, so what the heck.

I thought about my mother and what she'd say about blue hair, but all I could come up with were her words "Always wear clean underwear." She never warned me about hair color, so off we went.

That's when the guys appeared. I think they had been surreptitiously hiding under rocks or in their dorm rooms until that moment. Before now, hardly anyone had been on campus. We all forgot that this was the day thousands of college students were arriving. *Good timing, Alicia,* I thought to myself sarcastically.

That is how I met John—the cute college guy with the dark hair, incorrigible air, and playful grin who sauntered up in the middle of several friends and snickered at the blue-haired buffoons before him. I consoled one of my friends: "Don't worry! We will never see them again!"

The next night, Cornell sponsored a party for those of us in the summer program. They fashioned the entertainment after MTV's *Singled Out* show, where a blindfolded person ends up with a date for the night based on a series of ridiculous questions his partner has to answer. A friend and I walked into the room, and John stood up and yelled out, "Blue hair!" The *Singled Out* game was a great backdrop, as the entire room directed their attention to me. It's a good thing he did embarrass me, though—John and I have been together ever since.

If I had never followed a whim to dye my hair blue (which I immediately washed out after dinner that night), I would never have met John, my best friend and boyfriend. The one time I let loose and did something without caring what others thought about it, I had the time of my life.

Things could have ended up differently that day. I could merely have been the girl on the corner in khaki shorts, but that memory would have been fleeting and short-lived. There are thousands of people in college, and it takes something unusual to stand out among them. So I was the girl with blue hair. And to this day, I have never regretted it. The five minutes it took to spray my hair changed my life for the better.

And what does John have to say about the whole incident? He still makes fun of me, like when he told his mother how we met. Now his sister and brother-in-law know, and my parents eventually found out as well. But they all have the same reaction. They all laugh and say that is the funniest "first meeting" of a couple they have ever heard.

And despite the fact the blue hair led me to John, he has explicitly asked me not to dye my hair blue again. I promised him that I wouldn't. No, next time I'm definitely thinking pink.

ALICIA BILLINGTON

Alas! How enthusiasm decreases,
as our experience increases!
LOUISE COLET

WAITING FOR
DUSTIN HOFFMAN

hen I was fifteen, I saw the movie The Graduate
with my best girlfriend, Terri, and together we both
fell in love with Dustin Hoffman. We made a vow
that one of us would marry Dustin and live happily ever after in a
huge mansion in Hollywood with a swimming pool, oversized
closets, and maids. We'd heard that he was a New Yorker, but that
was just a minor detail. We were optimistic and in love; nothing
else mattered.

We knew Dustin was thirty and didn't see it as a problem.
There were many women who married older men. Someday we
would be twenty and he would be thirty-five, and that didn't
sound quite so bad. When we turned fifty, he would be sixty-five.
Besides, we were very mature for our age.

Terri and I also swore we'd always be best friends and we
wouldn't be jealous of each other. Whoever got Dustin was fine,
just as long as it was one of us.

We cut school one day and stayed at the movies until 5:00 P.M.
watching Dustin. By day's end, we knew the dialogue by heart.
"Plastics!" we both said at the appropriate time. "Are you trying to
seduce me, Mrs. Robinson?" we both said on cue and giggled.

I bought magazines and a construction worker's lunch box. I glued all of my magazine pictures of Dustin onto the lunch box and covered it with shellac. I spilled some shellac on the carpet in my bedroom and disguised it by rearranging my furniture while my mother was at work. I carried my Dustin box wherever I went. I thought it made a statement about who I was.

Then we heard that Dustin was going to star in an Off-Broadway play called *Jimmy Shine,* and of course we went to see it. Neither of us really paid much attention to the play. We were looking at Dustin's expressions. We were watching him move. We were in the same room as Dustin Hoffman. We were breathing air that might have gone through his lungs.

We left before the curtain calls, found the stage door, and planted ourselves right in front of it. We were the first ones there. A crowd formed around us. We became animals in order to keep our front spots, pushing people back. I was pushing people with my Dustin lunch box. One after another, theater people left, but there was no sign of Dustin Hoffman.

Terri began to panic. "What if we're at the wrong door!"

I began to hyperventilate. "What if he already left!"

Then the door opened and it was Dustin. He exited and he looked even better in person. I pushed my *Playbill* toward him. While he was signing my *Playbill,* my hand touched his. I had touched Dustin Hoffman. My skin had brushed his skin.

I didn't wash my hand for two weeks. I wore a glove long before Michael Jackson called himself the Gloved One. I took the glove off and stared at my fingers. My hand looked different now that it had touched Dustin. It looked older and more sophisticated.

One day, I picked up the Manhattan directory. It was a few years old. For some reason, I decided to look up Dustin Hoffman. It was there. Dustin Hoffman was listed in the Manhattan phone book. There was his name and his address and his telephone number. I tore the page out of the phone book, went to the phone and dialed Dustin's number. It rang a few times and then someone answered the phone.

"Hello," said the voice. It was Dustin Hoffman. I couldn't breathe.

"Hello," the voice at the other end of the phone repeated.

I hung up.

I was a mess. I had heard Dustin Hoffman on the phone. I had heard his voice. I had been electrically connected to him. I had been on the phone with the movie star I would someday marry. Then reality hit. I had just hung up on Dustin Hoffman. I picked up the phone again. I had to apologize and make it right. I redialed Dustin's number.

He answered the phone. "Hello?"

I tried to hide my shaking voice to say hello this time, but when I opened my mouth, nothing came out.

"Hello!" he said again. Now he was barking.

"Hello!" he shouted. "Who is it?" he yelled. Then he slammed the phone down.

I was miserable. I'd made Dustin Hoffman angry. I'd ruined everything.

Terri and I talked on the phone all night. I repeated the details of the two phone calls. She was furious because I called him. She said she didn't have a chance to hear him. She said that since I broke the pact, all was fair in love and war. Terri said that when she married Dustin Hoffman, she would never invite me to her mansion in Beverly Hills. I tried to calm her down. I didn't want my best friend to be so mad. I told her I had a better idea.

By 9:00 o'clock Monday morning, we were standing in front of Dustin Hoffman's brownstone apartment. We were in New York; we were cutting school again, but now that we were here, neither of us knew what to do next. There was a lot of giggling. There was a lot of discussion. Finally, we got brave. We walked up the stairs. We were holding hands and moving very slowly. We entered the vestibule to Dustin Hoffman's building. On one wall were buzzers with names next to them. There it was: "Hoffman, D." It was as simple and as innocuous as Smith, J., or Jones, L.

We stood there giggling. Then Terri got brave and pushed the button beside Dustin's name. Then we ran. We ran back outside and down the stairs. We were laughing and hysterical and crying and we just ran. When we finally stopped, we looked at each other, turned, started to laugh, and arm in arm we marched back to Dustin's apartment. We climbed the stairs once again, entered the vestibule, and bravely rang his buzzer. This time we waited. And we waited. No one was there.

We decided to get out of there. I put my hand on the label "Hoffman, D." for good luck. My nail accidentally slid under the label, and I peeled it off. I put my lips to the gummy label and kissed it. Then I put it in my pocket and we left.

Time moved on as it always does. Terri and I parted ways, and with it, my infatuation with Dustin Hoffman died. For that period in my life, I thought Dustin Hoffman was the reason I had to get up each day. With Terri gone, it was no longer important.

I think I remember hearing Dustin Hoffman in an interview mentioning that he no longer lived in New York, that for years he had sublet the apartment we once visited. He said nothing about the phone calls or the address label. He had no memory of a young girl's hand brushing his when he signed a *Playbill*.

FELICE R. PRAGER

*W*hat's wrong with me? Those were the words that rolled through my mind when my mom took me to a specialist to help me with my reading problem.

I'm thirteen, and through my years in school I never understood why spelling was so difficult, yet I loved to write. Listening came easy, but I never understood what I read. My grades were above average, and since I was quiet by nature, the teachers didn't notice that I was having difficulties.

My mom felt there was a problem when it took me three hours to do homework every night, even with her help. I began to hate school and kept my frustrations buried inside.

Mom complained to the teachers that they were giving too much homework, and they told her no other parents had voiced concern.

Reading out loud in class was embarrassing. If I made a mistake, students would yell out the word that I messed up and it sounded like everyone was yelling at me.

Finally, they recommended that I be tested by a psychologist. She diagnosed that I had a problem processing information, calling it a reading disability.

The psychologist wanted my parents to get me a tutor to help me catch up in reading and told me that I had to talk to my teachers and tell them to repeat something if I didn't catch it. Patience was the key. I needed to go slower in order to understand what I read.

The tutor worked with me in the summer, using flash cards to help me learn sounds, but even better, she helped me gain confidence in myself and allowed me to discover the ways that I am smart. My "enrichment" class at school taught me how to do homework and review for tests, and my teachers gave me extra time to do class work. Mom or Dad would read out loud from my textbooks at night so that I understood the lessons better.

The best thing that happened to me was finding my best friend, Katrina. She was the smartest girl in the class, and yet she still asked me for help! I felt my confidence grow even larger when I heard one of the girls dividing up the class into four groups. She pointed at Jacob, Adam, Katrina, Bobby, Jimmy, and me, and said, "Those kids should be known as the 'smarties' of our homeroom."

One day in science class, my teacher, Mrs. Menchaca, was talking about Albert Einstein, telling us he had dyslexia and that it was harder for him to process information, yet he turned out to be one of the greatest geniuses that ever lived. She said, "Nobody is perfect, so don't tease people, and don't be afraid to admit you have a problem."

Her words rolled through my body and settled there. Even though Einstein had a disability, he was one of the greatest geniuses who ever lived. And knowing that has changed me—and how I think about myself—forever.

SUZANNE BERTRAND

SPRING HARVEST

*H*is elegant tallith disguises his youth. He seems old, knowledgeable of all we desire to ask. We watch, wait, praying he won't falter, stumble over the well-rehearsed Hebrew prayers. Even though we all know he won't.

Mike has counted the days until this glorious moment. A bridge is being built between his youth and his adulthood, in the tightly knit Jewish community that has taught him the ageless lessons of our complex lives. His glossy brown eyes are a constant reminder of the childhood he has led. Like an eagle, he seems to watch us from the podium.

His mom, Rachel, sits happily in the front row. Her clasped hands rest on her creamy white skirt. A gentle smile tickles the corners of her thin lips. Beside her, Mike's dad, Tom, proudly watches the ceremony, his eyes glued to Mike. The twins Ben and Andrew, Mike's brothers, sit in awe. In all my twelve years, I have not seen them so still and silent. Focusing my attention back to Mike, I realize how much we have changed. Yet the bud of friendship still blossoms.

In the days when clouds were cotton candy and change seemed distant, Mike and I were friends from opposite ends of the pre-fifth-grade social chain in Berkeley. Somehow the "boys-have-cooties" routine didn't make sense to me. Unlike every other girl, I numbered guys as half of my "best" friends. Weird, isn't it?

I remember playing hide-and-go-seek with Mike, his brothers, and whoever else happened to be in the neighborhood. It was an energetic game with a twist of patience. The thought of sitting in leaf mush and splintery branches was overpowered by the thrill of secretly sneaking back to base. That was how it was in the spring. The season when the forgotten foliage was reborn and great new hiding spots were discovered. With crooked lines and orange crayons, Mike and I would map out all potential hiding places each and every year. Then the games would begin.

Before long, spring would draw back and summer would roll in. A new season would begin: baseball season. Accompanied by fresh balls, well-loved mitts, and a silver bat, Mike, Ben, Andrew, and I would troop down to Cragmont Park. A meadow surrounded by eucalyptus trees gracing the elegant houses of Berkeley. This would be our new field. With decided teams and understood rules, we would begin the game. Hours of pitching, batting, and disagreements between Mike and the twins crowned my summer days. Nervous neighbors would wearily watch our games, waiting for an uncontrolled ball to sail toward their cars baking in the sun. But nothing ever happened. Summer would soon be fleeing from us, with school nipping at its heels.

Auburn leaves twirled down from trees, covering our sidewalks. Jeans took over from shorts. Teachers seized our baseballs and replaced them with homework. Mike and I used to sit Indian-style on his blue-sheeted bed. School projects and yellow pencils lay at our fingertips. Halloween candy surrounded us in piles while we decided what to eat, save, and trade. Talk of the day we had led filled the room in soft voices, as we searched for what we had missed during the long hours at school.

The icy grasp of winter would then squeeze away all memories we had of the sun. Rain would flood the skies. I used to spend the night at Mike's house in the winter. At midnight, like spies, we would slip downstairs to the castle of food, the kitchen. Like starved children we would stuff ourselves with Triscuit sandwiches (crackers and cheese microwaved), challenging each other to build the tallest sandwich. Mike always won. In the morning, Rachel would put on a puzzled mask as she questioned us about "not being hungry for breakfast." But she always knew the truth.

Then spring came again. The season when the forgotten foliage was reborn and great new hiding spots were discovered. The cycle continued . . . and continued.

Here I am today. Celebrating the coming of age of Mike. Nine and a half years of friendship. Here he is, the same rambunctious child who used to play baseball with me. Age has shaped his soul but spared his personality.

His last words of prayer echo through the wooden rafters overhead. I watch as he steps down from the podium. The audience is still. Then with a sudden energy, they rise from the wooden benches, ready to congratulate Mike. Amazed and honored to have been a part of the ceremony, I watch him. Mike gracefully turns toward me. An instant of understanding flies between us floating on memories of cream-puff clouds.

"Good job," I mouth.

He smiles.

ALEXANDRA LEWIS

What really matters is what you do with what you have.
SHIRLEY LORD

THE PROOF IS IN THE PUDDING

G oing to college more than ten years out of high school was scary. I had filled out and submitted all the necessary paperwork, and two weeks later, a representative from the admissions office called to set up an appointment for me to see an admissions counselor. My heart pounded rapidly as I entered the counselor's office.

"Hello, Mrs. Lucio. Have a seat."

After some initial chitchat, he gave me the bad news.

"We've been reviewing your applications, and I'm sorry to tell you that we've decided to reject your application for admission to St. Mary's at this time. Why don't you take some classes at a community college and apply for admission at a later date?"

"Why was I rejected?" I asked.

"Well, our decision was based primarily on your ACT scores. Although you did very well on some subjects, you did poorly on others."

"What about my high school grades? I did well in high school."

"You've been out of school too long."

I was feeling let down, because going to college was something I was mentally prepared to do. Knowing this, I suggested that perhaps they could allow me to take the test over.

"That's not a good idea. You won't do well because you've been out of high school more than ten years. Besides, you're too old and will probably not be able to compete with the younger students."

His last words shattered my self-esteem. Not knowing what else to say, I muttered a quick "well, thanks anyway" and left, disappointed and dejected. To make matters worse, I knew my supervisor, Mrs. H, was waiting to hear the "good news." She had been encouraging me to continue my education throughout the years I'd been working with her at the university library.

Initially, her suggestion seemed outrageous. How could I possibly work full-time, be a mom and a wife, and go to college? I would politely nod in agreement, but I didn't take her advice seriously. Finally, it dawned on me that she was right. Although I hadn't yet decided what to major in, I made up my mind that I was ready to take college courses. After I had done all I was required to do, St. Mary's had turned me down.

"So what did they say?" asked Mrs. H.

"They rejected my application."

I told her everything the counselor had told me. She was upset, too, over what was said to me and got on the phone and spoke to another person from the admissions office.

"She has to go to school. I know she can do it," I overheard her say.

Who better than Mrs. H would know my actual capabilities, my learning and comprehension skills? Year after year, she had been evaluating my work as "Outstanding," recommending that I "Take the opportunity to further [my] education." The admissions counselor didn't know me, yet here he was saying that I wouldn't "be able to compete with the younger students."

The rejection hurt. I felt St. Mary's was saying I was good enough as an employee but not good enough to be one of their students. Their decision didn't make sense to me, but I concluded that if they didn't want me, I wasn't going to beg them.

The day after the terrible admissions office interview, I received a phone call from a woman in the evening studies office asking me to meet with her. She questioned me about my interest in going to school. I told her that it was something I wanted for myself— simply for the sake of learning, not just as a means to getting a better job.

"Look," she finally said, "we're going to accept you into the Evening Studies Program, but you'll be on probation for the first twelve hours of credit. You'll only be allowed to enroll in evening courses. If at any time during this period you get a grade lower than a 'C,' you will be suspended from the program."

As a result of the conditions put before me, I had the opportunity early on to prove that I could succeed, not fail as the counselor had predicted. Whenever the admission counselor's words, "You're too old and will probably not be able to compete with the younger students," rang in my ears, I'd counter it with, *You have to prove him wrong.*

I often felt insecure while taking those first twelve hours of credit, never uttering a word in class unless I was called on. Yet, two years later, I completed my probationary period with a grade-point average above a 3.5.

Sixteen years ago, an admissions counselor was able to intimidate me, but now I've taken all my confidence and self-esteem back.

To this day, I wonder about the real reason that the counselor did not consider my high school grades. Was my high school not prestigious enough in his eyes? If I could sit down with that same admissions counselor today, I would tell him to be careful how quickly he judges someone. But I don't have time right now because I've got some calls to make to order my cap and gown.

NETTIE R. LUCIO

BRICK BY BRICK

By the time I was eighteen years old, I was certain I'd never find love. I know eighteen seems like a young age, and it is, but I was convinced that I would spend the rest of my life alone.

I couldn't imagine creating a life with any of the guys I had dated so far. Like the guy who wouldn't commit to seeing just me, and eventually left me with a broken heart when I found out he had had another girlfriend all along. And the perfectly nice guy I went out with for two weeks, before I told him it wasn't working and broke his heart. I even had a long-distance relationship, which inevitably ended badly, as things like that tend to do.

Living in a small town and being painfully shy didn't help. I just didn't do well in social situations. I decided to take matters into my own hands. I placed a personal ad on the Internet. It may sound desperate, but it seemed like the perfect solution to me. This way I could let guys know exactly what I was looking for, and exactly what they'd get in me.

I got several replies immediately, but one caught my eye. His name was Mike, and he was still living at home, as I was. We both liked the same kinds of music, and we loved movies. Both of us admitted we were shy, but after writing back and forth for a couple of months, we decided to meet for dinner at a Chinese restaurant that was fairly close to where we both lived.

Unfortunately, the day we planned to meet was the day of the worst ice storm of the year. When we had to reschedule, I was secretly relieved. As much as I wanted to meet Mike, I worried that a blind date would be a lot harder than talking online.

The next time we were supposed to meet, I canceled at the last minute. I had a good excuse—I had to drive my dad someplace. But again I was relieved that I'd put off meeting Mike. When I wrote him to apologize for canceling yet again, he understood. We talked on the phone for the first time that night and set up our next date to meet. When I heard his sweet-sounding voice, I smiled. I could already tell something wonderful was trying to happen here.

The night we met in person, Mike picked me up at my door and drove us to the restaurant, and even opened doors for me. I'd never gone out with anyone with good manners before! From the moment I set eyes on him, I was smitten. During dinner we talked about our hobbies and friends. Mike did most of the talking during dinner, since I was so tongue-tied. After dinner, he paid for our meals, which was another first, and then drove me home.

The first thing I did after getting in was to call my best friend. She was worried at first that the date was over so soon. I assured her everything was fine.

"He's a really nice guy," I told her. "I thought he was cute, and I'd love to go out with him again."

"That's great!" she replied.

She convinced me to write him and tell him that I'd like to do it again sometime. I told him I'd try to be more talkative the next time we went out. When I got Mike's reply, he said he would try not to be as shy either. We set up a second date for Saturday.

The week was a blur up until Saturday night. I was excited. I couldn't wait to see Mike again. Mike picked me up at my house, and it still amazed me when he opened the car door for me. The theater was packed. Apparently a lot of other people had the same idea he did. I didn't know what movies were playing, but Mike had one in mind already. I waited while he paid for the tickets (another first for me). When he returned with two tickets for *Shakespeare in Love*, I was astonished. This was a typical chick flick.

When Mike drove me home, we said good night at the door. I watched him walk back to his car and my heart melted. I was in love, no doubt about it!

The only problem was, it was way too soon to tell Mike that. I'd made the mistake before of saying "I love you" too early, and it felt empty afterward when the other person didn't care. So I promised myself I'd take it slow with Mike. Wait and see.

We talked to each other on the Internet every day after that. Even if we hadn't decided to date, I think we would have been good friends. I couldn't help myself, though: I told him in a letter that I wished I had worked up the nerve to kiss him good night after our second date. To my surprise, he expressed the same regret. We were both too shy.

After our third date, we stood on the porch talking for a while even though it was freezing outside. We talked about constellations, and our respective childhoods. Mike is an only child, and I have a younger brother, so I had plenty of amusing anecdotes to share. He kept saying he should go, but he wasn't in any hurry. We were just enjoying each other. We unconsciously stood closer to each other every time we moved. The next thing we knew, we were kissing. Our first kiss was magical. I think I'll remember that moment forever. It seemed like every other person ceased to exist, and this instant was all that mattered. When we finally separated, I was smiling from ear to ear. Mike grinned back at me saying, "I'm not cold anymore." After we exchanged our goodbyes and made plans to see each other again, he left.

I spent my days looking forward to seeing Mike again and my nights dreaming of him. We just seemed to click, as though we were made for each other. Some dates we just spent the evening in my TV room, watching movies and holding hands until 2:00 A.M. Yet, as much as it seemed that I had found my soul mate, I was still wary. There was always that little voice inside my head saying, "He doesn't really like you."

One day when we were making plans to go to a movie that

evening, Mike said the most awful words I'd ever heard. "There's something I want to talk to you about later." I was horrified. Wasn't that just the way to tell me things weren't working?

He picked me up, and we went to the movie, but I could barely concentrate on the film, because I was worried about what he had to say. The car ride back to my house was mostly silent. I was beginning to think he had forgotten, and I wasn't about to bring it up. When we arrived at my house, I was about to go inside, when he finally spoke his mind. "There's something I have to tell you," he began. I just nodded. "I've never met anyone like you before, and I think we have something very special."

At first I couldn't speak. "I feel the same way about you, too." I smiled.

We shared a hug and kissed goodnight. "I love you, Sarah," he said softly.

My heart soared hearing him say those words. I didn't hesitate to voice the feelings I'd been having for some time now. "I love you too, Mike." And as I closed the door and went inside, I knew I had found my true love.

From that point on, we spent every moment we could together. We talked of the future, mine and his, and ours. Two people, each wanting the best for the other, making us stronger together than if we were apart. He encouraged me to continue my education, and helped me realize my love for computers. We've outlined a plan for how we'll eventually buy a house and have kids.

So here I am almost two years after our first date, and Mike and I are engaged. I'm attending college full-time, working toward a degree in computer information systems, and Mike is a graphic designer. Our plan is to get married as soon as I've graduated. I can't wait. Some people say we're just lucky. But luck has nothing to do with it. We're reaping the rewards of taking it slow and easy. Mike and I are both busy laying a strong foundation, brick by brick, made out of mutual love, friendship, encouragement, and respect—ingredients that will sustain us for a lifetime and shelter us through any storm that comes our way.

SARAH HORST

MY FRONT MAN

*S*tanley *and I have grown up together, and he now rests high up in my closet, in a large vaudeville, travel case.*

When I was a little girl I used to go to my aunt Sondra and uncle Al's house to visit. While playing one afternoon in my cousin Gary's room, I found a Charlie McCarthy puppet and a record album by Jimmy Nelson titled *Instant Ventriloquism*. I parked myself in front of a mirror with Charlie, and I knew right away that I was destined to be a ventriloquist.

I went home and asked my mom if she'd take me to the toy store so I could get an inexpensive puppet of my own to practice with. I became quite good at talking with my mouth closed and creating funny voices, so I saved my money and bought a used, professional ventriloquist figure from a magician down South.

Stanley arrived in the mail with a change of clothes, a half-eaten bag of chocolate chip cookies, and a note that read, "I sent the cookies in case Stanley got hungry on his trip."

Right away Stanley learned to mimic the television ads for Nestlé Quik like the puppet on the screen, sing songing, "N-e-s-t-l-e-s, Nestlé's makes the very best . . . chaaawc-late!" I'd stand in front of the mirror with Stanley repeating over and over again, "The boy bought a basketball," with my mouth closed. After I mastered that feat, I felt I could do anything!

At first, Stanley was just a ventriloquist figure, something to play with, but as the years rolled by, he soon became my friend and confidant.

During those awkward teenage years when I wasn't quite so sure of myself, I was lucky to have Stanley around. Before long, I realized that he had the courage to say things I couldn't and he'd stand up for what he believed in when I wouldn't. In embarrassing situations, I definitely allowed Stanley to have his say.

He loved to go out with me, and he soon became my front man. One time at a party when I didn't have the nerve to tell my boyfriend it was over, Stanley broke up with him for me!

I seem to find less and less time for Stanley these days, but it's comforting to know he is still around like a wise old sage. Recently, on his birthday, I lifted him down from the closet shelf so that I could thank him for being my front man for so long. He looked at me, winked, and said, "You had it in you all along."

KIM CHAMPION

V
PATHWAYS

There are many trails up the mountain,
but in time they all reach the top.

ANYA SETON

SAMMY

Sammy and I met in *Advanced Biology* our senior year in high school. I was sixteen, almost seventeen, and couldn't wait until June and graduation, which in September of 1964 seemed a hundred years away. I hated high school and was only there because I needed that diploma in order to get into college. It hadn't yet occurred to me that college was school too; I saw it only as a ticket out of Miami and away from home. I was going to the Colorado I had seen in the movies, and I couldn't wait to start life over again in a place where no one knew me.

Sammy strolled casually into class only seconds before the bell rang and gracefully folded his long frame into the other seat of the big double desk I had staked out in the very back of the room. He was tall and lanky with a big goofy smile in an otherwise earnest face.

"So I guess this means we're to be lab partners this year. I'm Sammy." He stuck out his hand for me to shake. I stared at his hand and then at him.

"I hear we get to dissect fetal pigs at the end of the year. I can't wait." He grinned, ignoring my lack of response. The thought of cutting up a pig repulsed me beyond belief, but truthfully, I would have butchered anything to avoid taking Chemistry, the only science alternative.

Just then Mr. Gordon, our teacher, came in wearing the most amazing tie I had ever seen, so wide it almost covered his entire pudgy chest. It was decorated with large brightly painted parrots. Surely it must have glowed in the dark. The class sat in stunned silence. Except for Sammy, who emitted a loud, "Wow!" Then everyone erupted in helpless laughter. I looked over at Sammy and smiled tentatively at him. Maybe the year would be bearable after all.

When not in school, I spent every waking moment at the stables. My love of horses and years of hard work and lessons had won me a little recognition in the saddle-horse circle of South Florida. Afternoons and weekends were spent working horses, being trained, teaching beginning riders, and traveling to horse shows. There was no time for "normal" teen activities or dating. Not that there was much chance of that anyway—I was much too shy. Horses were easier to relate to than people were. Still, I longed for friends and I was convinced that once in Colorado I'd magically turn into another person.

Other than seeing him every Monday through Friday at 7:30 A.M. in class, I never gave Sammy a thought. Side by side we mutilated starfish and frogs, the smell of formaldehyde burning our eyes.

Spring finally brought Sammy's longed-for pigs. We named ours Petunia and devoted the next three weeks of our lives to dismantling her. While we were chipping away, Sammy invited me to the prom. "Why not," I replied, concentrating on not touching anything that was actually part of Petunia.

At that moment we became inseparable. So much so that while I was visiting my mother nearly twenty years later and being introduced to an elderly woman at her church, the woman peered into my face and said, "Why, you're Sammy's Mary."

As the weeks passed and the horses I worked were sold in preparation for my leaving for college, the hours that had been consumed by horses were now filled with Sammy. The girl who had never had a best friend or a boyfriend now had both. We met early mornings at Royal Castle, taking our 15-cent hamburgers and 5-cent root beers to Biscayne Bay, where we'd walk along the water's edge, hastily brushing the sand from between our toes before rushing off to class.

Then suddenly it was the beginning of that seemingly endless humid summer, when the air was so thick you could watch it and every single time you turned on the radio they were playing the Beatles' "Help." We wound up seeing the movie seven times together, each time laughing until our stomachs hurt. We took Sammy's father's boat out into the ocean and explored islands so tiny even I could toss a shell clear to the other side. We collected sand dollars and sea biscuits, brown and furry, from the ocean's shallow pools. And we took long drives in his father's new Chrysler, stopping at gas stations for RC Colas, which we'd shake up and spray at each other.

On moonlit nights we'd walk through the Australian pines along the miles of narrow winding sandy trails leading eventually to the ocean's edge and the abandoned lighthouse. There we'd sit on the seawall, dangling our feet over the ocean, watching the thousands of glittery lights floating in the seaweed. Sammy said they were really minute sea life, but they looked like tiny stars to me. The wind whispering through the Australian pines made a soft, faraway murmuring sound, lonesome and melancholy.

After such nights I'd lie on my bed, the humid air so heavy I could feel it resting on my skin. Feelings of sadness and shame would waft over me and I'd feel lonely and confused. But then Sammy would call, and I'd marvel again that someone so wonderful could like me so much. Once we fell asleep listening to each other breathe into the phone.

Fifteen years later, Sammy would ask me what had happened to us. "I always thought we'd eventually get married and spend the rest of our lives being a couple of happy dumb slobs together." By then he was married with a son who looked just like him. I didn't know how to explain that I never believed I deserved him. He was just too clean and good. It would be another ten years before I would finally understand it wasn't me who was bad, it was the man who molested me during all the years he was teaching me to train horses.

On August 24, 1992, Hurricane Andrew began marching relentlessly across South Florida with wind gusts of more than 175 miles an hour, taking lives, homes, and every single tree with it. When phone service was at last restored, I was relieved to hear my mother's calm voice answer the phone same as always. Before she hung up, she said she had talked to Sammy. "He said one of the biggest losses for him was that he'd never hear the Australian pines again."

I'll always hear them in my heart, Sammy. My biggest loss is that it took me so long to see myself as you always had—clean and good.

MARY ZELINKA

*R*ecently, *my granddaughter was telling me about a* new girl in her school.

"She doesn't speak good English, and the other kids think she is strange, Nana," Nichole told me. "The teacher asked me to try and make friends with her. The teacher says the girl, her name is Maria, needs a new friend to show her around."

"Your teacher is a wise, caring woman, and I hope you will try and do as she suggested," I said. "Maria probably feels pretty strange and scared. It's hard being the new girl, especially if you don't speak the language well. Put yourself in her shoes, and see how you would feel if you were the new girl." Then I told her about being the new, strange girl in my school, a long time ago. New girls felt the same then as they do today.

When I started school in my new country, the United States of America, in January of 1952, I was classified as a Displaced Person. And at fifteen, "displaced" described both my legal status and my fragile self-esteem. My family and I had lived through World War II, in our country, Hungary, followed by four years in a refugee camp. The relatively carefree life that our new country presented us with took some getting used to.

So there I was—a mousy, shy, D.P. girl who spoke with a thick accent and was barely acknowledged by her beautiful American peers. For beautiful is what they were to me, those girls with their ponytails, bobby socks, and carefree, laughing ways, and I longed to be just like them. But I was different; my past still haunted me.

The school I attended was an all-girls school run by nuns, and girls who attended came from all parts of the city we lived in, the older girls driving their cars to get there. We lived in a small rental house near the school, so I walked to it. I was aware that it was a great sacrifice for my grandparents to send me there, since money was still scarce in our household and the school had a tuition and uniform and book expenses. And I felt lucky to have been accepted, since my English was still not up to par. One of my Hungarian friends had not been so lucky, and had been placed back in the sixth grade. Mortified, she soon quit school and got a job in a sewing factory.

By the time June rolled around, I had been in my new school six months. I was still shy and mousy, and barely noticed by the other girls, but despite my poor academic performance, they passed me to the tenth grade. I was relieved. I spent that first summer in America working part-time at our local dime store and hanging out with Hungarian friends at the beach.

Good things always end much too soon, and in September of that year, it was time to don the old blue and gold jumper and white blouse again and go back to school. Of course, I entered the building with trepidation, and although some of the girls greeted me cheerily, I had not turned into a swan over the summer, and I was quite aware of that. Then I walked into Sister Mary Ann's sophomore English class, and soon everything changed.

Sister Mary Ann had the bluest eyes, a smile that lit up the classroom, and a gentle, sympathetic, understanding manner. She recognized my pain, and began asking me about my life in front of the class. It was so that my classmates could better understand why I was different from them, she explained, and gently implored them to put themselves in my shoes and see how they would feel in them. My mind soon concluded that an angel had come into my life! Then the good sister gave us our first assignment of the new school term.

"I want you all to write an essay of at least four pages about something memorable that has happened to you. It will be due a week from today." When we left her classroom, I wasn't too sure I knew what an essay was, but for the first time at that school, I put my heart and soul into an assignment.

I wrote about being crammed, with hundreds of other hopeful refugees, on a ship taking us to our new country. I wrote about Dave, the young American who befriended me and brought me my first Coke. I wrote about my first sight of the Statue of Liberty and about being tagged and ushered for processing to the main building of Ellis Island, into an enormous hall filled with throngs of bewildered people. And I realized that I liked writing.

The day after we handed in our essays, Sister Mary Ann had me read mine to the class. To my surprise, my classmates applauded when I finished. Then I was sent to read it throughout the school and got the same reaction. Girls mobbed me in the hallway telling me how much they liked my essay, asking me questions, paying attention to me. Suddenly, I was more than just that mousy D.P. girl; I was being accepted as one of them. Because of a caring teacher, the culture shock was broken, and to that gentle soul in the blue and white habit, I shall always be grateful.

RENIE SZILAK BURGHARDT

There's a time when one more word
ruins the story, one more step ruins the dance.
AUTHOR UNKNOWN

CHOREOGRAPHING A LIFE

*F*or a variety of reasons, both physical and philosophical, I ended up moving on to my second career at twenty-one when most of my friends were still trying to match up their liberal arts education to something in the "real world" job market. At twenty-one, I had seventeen years of training and experience in the world of professional ballet.

Knowing that I was going to make a break from dance to pursue writing, editing, and teaching left me with a hollow feeling in the pit of my stomach. I chastised myself for wasting my parent's money and my entire life since the age of four on something totally useless to me in the future. Or so I thought.

The summer I graduated from college, I suited up in my three-piece black silk ensemble so many times that I thought it would come apart at the seams before any of the countless job interviews I went to paid off. I cried and sweated my way from publishing house to publishing house on Manhattan's sweltering Avenue of the Americas.

As I trudged along, I was surprised to find myself thinking about times in ballet class when I had fallen on my face. Usually I fell while trying to do a step like my friend Jayne, who always did everything better. I remembered the rush of hard-earned pride when I'd finally get the step right after what seemed like endless attempts and failures. I felt rewarded for my efforts—and nothing but disdain for instant gratification.

Anything I wanted, including a publishing job, I'd get if I worked hard enough for it. And so I put on the suit, again and again.

In my very first interview, I came face to face with a man twice my height who looked like he never took his pin-striped suit and red power tie off. I wanted nothing more than to curl up on the floor of his office and die. At that same time, I recalled all the times I'd been faced with a difficult bit of choreography on stage. My teachers always told me that if I looked poised—if I looked like I hadn't made a mistake—then no one in the world would know whether I performed the choreography correctly or not.

The power-tie editor in chief offered me a chair, and I sat down, holding my back straight and my head high. I held his piercing stare while I answered his questions with a strong, clear, even-toned voice. The interview progressed, and he began to look at me like I knew what I was doing, as if I were capable and confident (when I was neither!).

This acknowledgment from him gave me the confidence I needed to keep going with my performance. That job ended up going to someone already working with the company, but the editor in chief did say when he called to deliver the bad news that he had never in his life seen such a poised and articulate twenty-one-year-old. "Those qualities will take you far," he declared. Despite my nonexistent employment status, I began to suspect that he was right. And that I had ballet to thank for it.

Three months later, I finally had a work phone number in one of the entry-level cubicles at a prominent educational publishing house, and I was ecstatic. I still had a long way to go getting used to spending eight hours a day in front of a computer with the phone cradled in the crook of my neck. In contrast, my most recent dance schedules had called for two hours in the studio, two on the tour bus, one in the dressing room, and the rest on stage without having to say a word to anyone.

I still had a lot of editing skills, corporate politics, and market savvy to master, although by then I knew that I would make it and that, strange as it sounds, ballet had ensured my success in my second field.

Every day since, I've encountered one obstacle or another where the solution, once I find it, can be traced back to the persistence, poise, and commitment I learned at the barre. Sure, it's true that executing perfect *fouetté* turns will never again land me a gig, but learning how to do those terrifying turns has given me everything I value today.

PAOLA JUVENAL

NOTES FROM HOME

My life has been blessed with two wonderful children, my son Ron and my daughter Marly. Like their father, I was raised in Europe and China before coming to America, and I brought a good bit of my background into their lives. Perhaps the fifties and sixties were an easier time to raise children than more recent times. All I can say is that I am glad that I had my kids in a more gentle, a more private time.

It didn't take me long to figure out that if I wanted to know what went on in my children's lives, and what kind of people their friends were, I would have to stick around and make the family home their playground. It was the best thing I have ever done. From kindergarten to college, we kept an open house for our children and their friends.

Winter evenings were spent in front of a big fire in the spacious den, consuming tons of spaghetti or devouring thick slices of pizza or rich slabs of lasagna. There was good talk, good music, and games galore. And on those long summer evenings, our children and their pals gathered on the patio. On the grill, hot dogs or hamburgers sizzled, and mountains of potato salad and pickles disappeared with astonishing speed. Once in a while, someone brought a guitar and a mini songfest made its way into the night. Best of all, I *knew* where our kids were. And, shame on me, I usually knew what they thought.

Ever so often, this close-knit group of kids would ask me to join them and tell stories about my checkered past—in Europe, in Shanghai—and the three years I spent with my parents and many other Jewish families in a Japanese detention camp—so different from their All-American lifestyles.

It was the summer of high school graduation. Soon, the Jackson Street Five, as the kids called themselves, would scatter in all directions as they entered the colleges of their choice.

The lengthy conversations Marly and her friends conducted were all about college and the dumb boys, clothes and the dumb boys, and lots of philosophizing about life and the dumb boys. On one particular night, their male friends had not joined them, and the young women added the subject of sex to their stream of chatter. Bits of their chitchat and bursts of carefree laughter drifted into the den where I was reading. Suddenly, the screen door squeaked open, and Mollie, one of my daughter's friends, stood in front of me, a serious expression on her face.

"Mrs. Lansing," she asked, "could you please help us answer a serious question?"

I nodded a silent yes.

"We want you to give us *your* definition of sex."

Well, things were getting serious out there under the starry, dark-blue Colorado sky. Mollie, at seventeen, had been dating steadily for more than two years and was lovingly looked upon as the femme fatale of the group. Could it be that in spite of all her "experiences" she did not feel qualified to define the subject for her friends? Both my children had their sex education before they entered kindergarten. Quite matter-of-factly, we discussed what needed to be discussed, giving the subject no more importance than the subject of good manners.

I was pleased these young people wanted my opinion on a subject about which I couldn't have questioned adults when I was Mollie's age.

"Well, girls," I started out, "I know you know the mechanics of the subject matter, so I'll keep it simple. Here it is: 'Sex is one more grand thing two married people do together, who already are doing everything else *well* together. Sex is no less, no more.' "

Although we talked a bit more about the subject, I couldn't be sure that *my* definition of sex had sunk in.

Six weeks later, I attended "Mother's Day" at Colorado State University, where my daughter had started her freshman year. Looking for the place to freshen up and powder my nose, Marly directed me to the dorm's "lavatory."

Upon entering the large, communal room reeking of a hodge-podge of hairsprays, soaps, and toilet articles, my eyes fell onto a large bulletin board. Tacked to it with a yellow stick pin—amid lost curlers, announcements for events, books to share, and requests for rides to various locations—was a piece of white paper. Written on it in purple ink, in my daughter's round handwriting, were the following words:

"Sex is one more grand thing two married people do together, who already are doing everything else *well* together. Sex is no less, no more."

By my mother.

—Marly Lansing

Ursula Bacon

THE FINAL SPRINT

*K*aty Byrne was born with the adrenaline of athletic competition running through her blood. She was
raised in a family where sports, competition, and physical exertion were facts of life, as natural as daily meals. Her summer weekends are for Windsurfing, trail hiking, and tennis. In the
evenings, she plays cutthroat soccer games where she enjoys
crushing anyone who dares to get in the way of her and the ball.

Then there's me. I was born with the warm milk of sleepy con-
templation running through my blood. Raised in a family where
sports are only practiced on TV, competition is limited to the
classroom, and physical exertion is to be avoided like the plague,
I'm the kind of woman who spends summer weekends napping,
reading and watching movies. Evenings find me in front of the
television, power-loafing, ready to crush anyone who dares to get
in the way of my time with a pint of ice cream and my date with
the couch.

Katy knows this. We've been friends since junior high. I may
prefer the movies to a soccer field, but there's one activity we can
agree on: meeting for coffee. So one sunny Saturday afternoon in
June, we sat outdoors at a wire-mesh table shaded by a giant umbrella and talked over iced coffee and lemonade.

"Heather and Kristi and I are doing the Starlight tonight," Katy
said, referring to the 5K evening "fun run" held downtown—a
run she'd participated in nearly every year since toddlerhood.
"You should come," she continued casually. "I might go out after.
I haven't decided yet." Katy took a sip of her cold drink and stared
across the parking lot.

"I want to go."

Katy snapped to attention, putting her drink down. "What?"

"I want to do Starlight with you."

"Are you serious?" Katy gave a couple of wide-eyed blinks. Her amazement wasn't surprising; after all, this was me we were talking about. Forcing myself to attend a few aerobics classes to assuage excess-pizza guilt doesn't exactly set a precedent for running a 5K.

"Yeah, I'm serious."

"Great! That's great! We'd love to have you." Katy gave me a big smile, obviously pleased that I had agreed to come. I smiled back, but my stomach was doing flip-flops.

What was I thinking? I suppose I wanted to feel like an athlete. Okay, so I'd been working out a little, hadn't I? Didn't I force myself off the couch occasionally and get my butt to the gym? Well, then, today I could do something even better: start and finish my first real race.

Hours later, wearing new workout clothes and my official Starlight T-shirt, I was ready for the race to begin. I stood waiting with Katy's friend Kristi, another mere mortal suckered into this crazy scheme, and Katy and her sister, Heather. Katy and Heather were "real" runners who ate people like Kristi and me for breakfast.

"Let's stand in the back of the crowd," I said, pointing to the race signs designating where the slower runners should stand. If they had a "wheezers" zone, I didn't see it. The four of us moved to the back.

I hopped around, stretching and bouncing in nervous anticipation. The race announcer told us that the course wasn't actually a 5K this year, but a little longer, more like 3.5 miles. Great, I thought. I'll be a gasping puddle of sweat after the first mile, and he's telling us the race has been extended to three and a half?

Katy explained that the important thing was not to get picked up by the bus that drives behind the runners, waiting to collect anyone who slows down enough to potentially collide with the parade that follows the race route. I tried to decide which was scarier: getting run over by a giant parade float or having to climb on board a bus designated for Runners Who Are Too Slow. Then again, if I got tired, the bus might start to look good. I checked behind me. No bus yet, but then again, we hadn't started.

The race began suddenly, and a cheer went up from the crowd. I was bouncin'. I was ready to go. I was stuck in the back.

It took almost two minutes before the wave of people waiting to race cleared the starting area and I was moving. Kristi and Heather jogged side by side, and Katy and I jogged behind them. It was exciting—the cool night air, the beauty of the city, the thrill of the race. I was ready to go faster, but the four of us were keeping a moderate, steady pace, so I adjusted to the rhythm and enjoyed myself.

For the first half mile.

The race got harder fast. Miraculously, although we didn't speed up, our light jog became a pounding run. Conversation was breathy and gasping, my face a pool of red heat. No matter what, though, I was determined not to hold the rest of the group back. Katy had been nice enough to invite me along, and I wasn't going to blow it for everyone. I maintained my wheezing pace and praised God when the group slowed to a walk.

At last we were almost to the finish line. Katy and Heather glanced at each other apprehensively, then at Kristi and me. Kristi and I had settled into a slow and painful trot that was trying to pass as a jog.

"Do you mind if we run the rest of the way?" Katy asked hesitantly. Kristi and I didn't mind. I think her knees were bothering her. Every fiber of my body was bothering me.

"Eeeh," I whimpered, waving a hand in the direction of the finish line, indicating that they should go ahead without us.

The two sisters took off like a shot, steel calves and iron thighs flexing, racer's arms pumping. The Starlight "fun run" was a high-school track competition again, and Katy and Heather were fighting for first place. They raced nose-to-nose toward the finish line, and at that moment I knew: Next year, I would run next to Katy during her final sprint. Her eyes would widen, her heart would race, and she would pick up speed, realizing that somewhere along the way, her couch-loving friend had become an athlete.

Kristi and I made it across the finish line a couple of minutes later to the cheers of Katy and Heather. We drank water, laughed, and savored the moment. I pictured next year in my mind and smiled.

It's May now, nearly a year later, and I'm psyched for the big day. I've been working out regularly, forcing myself to do more than my favorite step aerobics class. Now I actually jog, too. I'm still a sweaty, achy mess who'd rather be eating ice cream, but now I've found more motivation than keeping off the pounds: I have a race to run. I feel inspired. I do an exaggerated jog around the house, humming the theme from *Rocky*.

"I'm going to have T-shirts made," I tell my friends. "They'll say, 'This is the year! Beat a Byrne!' " Of course, Katy's got a lifetime of training behind her, and I've got only some practice on the treadmill, so I'm more likely to end up a Susan Lucci of the race world: deserving and tenacious, but waiting for years before I can claim a victory.

That's okay. It's not really the possibility of winning that inspires my newfound inner athlete. It's the thrill of the final sprint.

ALAINA SMITH

*A*fter bouncing around between two families for thirteen years, I consider myself an expert on seeing the bright side of having one mom, two dads, three sets of grandparents and lots of cousins. The good news is that I love them all.

My parents divorced each other when I was two years old. I don't remember that. My mom got married again to Tommy when I was five years old, and I do remember this. So for a long time, I've had two families, and I consider myself lucky.

All the grownups in my family love me. I have a very lovable dad, a very, loving mom, and a very caring stepdad. That's why I'm lucky. My dad and Tommy get along well. I like having two dads—it's great. They are very different in many ways, which makes it interesting. But one way they are similar is that Dad likes to be silly, and Tommy has a good sense of humor.

Sometimes my mom and dad get mad at each other about things that involve me, but mostly they agree. When I was younger, it sort of bothered me when they had disagreements, but now I think they are just having a hard time working out something and it will pass. I know they both love me, and that's what I care about. My dad pays for my piano lessons and makes me practice all the time, and he buys me new clothes. My mom makes me do chores around the house and keep my room clean and help out with my little brother Sean. Tommy likes us to do artwork together, and he takes me with him when he does things like go to the store or walk in the park or go out in the boat.

I split my time between two homes, and in each one, I have my own bedroom. At Mom and Tommy's house, my room has kind of an ocean theme, and at my dad's house it is sort of pink-ish and feminine.

With all the families in my life, I get to do lots of fun things. My dad is Dutch, so I went to Holland with him when I was twelve and met my cousins. I go to lots of family picnics, birthdays, and celebrations. Last week we had a surprise party for Tommy's birthday, and last summer I went to Washington State with my dad for a big family reunion.

My dad loves the mountains, and we go climbing and camping in beautiful places. Tommy is a ranger and lifeguard. He works on an island and in the ocean, so I am a junior lifeguard, go sailing, and spend lots of time at the beach swimming and boogie-boarding. My mom works at a botanical garden and loves the forest, so she likes to take us places like Yosemite and Sequoia National Park. I like to go to all these beautiful places.

When I was younger, the hardest thing was when two family events were at the same time and I had to choose—or Mom and Dad chose for me—which one to go to. I used to feel like I was missing something no matter what I did. Now I don't mind so much because I know I will have a chance to do something else with them another time. Like this week, my mom and Tommy and my brother are going out to Anacapa Island. I wanted to go, but my dad is a firefighter and just got back from Montana and was going on a climbing trip and wanted me to go. I wanted to be with him, too, because I was missing him, and I also wanted to go to the island. My mom and dad talked and decided that this time I would be with my dad.

On holidays I celebrate at Mom's house, Dad's house, and all three of my grandparents' houses. That's too much fun for one person!

I have friends whose parents are divorced, and things aren't as good for them. I wish their parents could get along better. One of my friends has a dad who used to live far away but now lives close by. He still never sees my friend, and she says she does not even like her dad. I suppose it's not perfect with my blended families; we do have some problems, but mostly I'm very happy with how everyone has worked things out.

At times, I try to get my way by asking my mom or dad about somewhere I want to go or something I want to buy, and if one says no, I'll ask the other. Sometimes it works, sometimes it doesn't. They usually agree with each other about what is best for me. Rats!

So with all this bouncing around, I've learned a few things. As I see it, two families are twice as much fun, I get to go twice as many places, and best of all, I get twice as much love!

KELSEY FEKKES

The way to achieve a difficult thing
was to set it in motion.
KATE O'BRIEN

MY HIGH-TECH WORLD

*W*hen I was working as a cashier at a supermarket, while most of my friends were in college, an
outspoken customer challenged me one day.

I was innocently sliding a can of soup across the scanner when
this woman said out of the blue, "You can't work here forever!
Where will you be in five years?"

I looked at her, mildly stunned. "I know." I stammered, "I'm
working on my writing and all this is helping with the bills."

She smiled, satisfied with my answer, and wished me good
luck.

For days afterward I thought about that encounter. Where *did* I
want to be in five years? I loved writing and art; my joy was in creative work. I kept a journal, but I hadn't written anything for pub-
lication and wasn't even trying.

A few weeks later, my best friend Donald phoned. I hadn't
heard from him for a while and was surprised when he told me
he'd bought a new computer. *So that's why he's disappeared lately!* I
thought.

"I want you to see a page I found, it's so funny!" He gushed.
"Come on over and hang out with me, we can write e-mail and
check out some message boards, too."

That was my introduction to the Internet.

I never pictured myself sitting in front of a glowing box all day as a career goal, but I soon realized that this could be the key to my using my creative talent. The Internet would allow me to write, design, create artwork, learn new skills, and participate in chats and discussions with others who shared my passions.

Since I was living with my mother and surviving on a cashier's salary, I couldn't afford a computer, so I bought a Web TV. It was a lot less than a computer, but it still allowed me to surf, communicate through e-mail, and learn HTML.

I spent every free moment soaking in information, writing codes, and animating my first Web site with an array of graphics that blinked, bobbed, danced, and flashed. The question remained: Could I make a career out of all this?

In a strange twist of fate, I heard about an opportunity at Web TV. Although it was a bit scary jumping right in, I had nothing to lose! I borrowed money, sold CDs and books to pay for my trip, and went to California to interview. Miraculously, I got the job as a temporary tech-support specialist for WebTV Networks. Suddenly I was making more than twice my salary at the supermarket in New York and learning what life was really like in a high-tech company.

I was struck a terrible blow when I found out that WebTV was no longer in need of my services. I went back to New York with a heavy heart, because to progress in new media, I needed the capabilities of a computer. After a time of wallowing in self-pity, I decided that I was going to make this work, and buying a "real" computer needed to be my next step.

Through savings and a little help, I was able to purchase a computer. I joined a mailing list for women in technology and answered an ad for an unpaid internship at a teen girls' community site. I was now entering a new field: Internet community.

I was soon working on other community sites as a moderator while still holding down my internship. I hosted chats and message boards on prestigious sites for an excellent salary, and I was having a lot of fun. What I once thought would be a boring career became brighter every day. The teen girls' site began paying me for my time as well. I balanced both jobs, working on as many as four sites at once and upwards of sixty hours a week. Now Donald wondered where I was!

A little over a year later, I was asked to become the manager of the site where I'd interned. I was ecstatic! This opportunity meant more responsibility, more money, and more fun. I now write a monthly column for a sister site, work with a fantastic team of people, and manage an intern plus five moderators. Feeling grateful has taken on a deeper meaning for me.

I have a new respect for myself because I chose a field and followed a path, which brought me to my natural place. There have been times when I've thought of the customer at the supermarket who challenged me by asking where I'd be in five years. I wish I could tell her that I wake up each morning thankful and excited about the day to come, absolutely in love with my work. As Martha Grimes once said, "We don't know who we are until we see what we can do."

Looking back, I see that not every journey is a straight line. Mine was a winding road taking me to a destination I had in mind. One determined step in front of the other eventually led me to where I most needed to be.

MAUREEN A. BOTHE

IF KHAKI'S GROOVE

If khaki's groove,
as the ad proclaims,
then trees spire
and lips christen
and geraniums
murmur bright
into the moonlight

so I'm thinking
khaki's do groove
and life moves
to the beat
of stars

and life is cool,
hooked up,
when you know
flowers glow
like moons
within us,
like drums
that sound
the way,

forever signaling
the beat, the tone,

the flow
that we might
match it,
simply match
the music in us
and move into
a greater zone.

SHEILA STEPHENS

VI
WATCHING OVER ME

Get quiet and let God talk to your heart.

AUTHOR UNKNOWN

A good message will always find a messenger.
AMELIA E. BARR

A SPECIAL DELIVERY

*T*he rain came down in sheets as I stood on the out-side platform of the High Barnet station just north of London. I was supposed to be headed for an interview for a terrific job at a prestigious company, but I hadn't mastered the transportation matrix yet and had inadvertently taken the wrong train. The next one wouldn't be along for at least twenty minutes, so I knew I would be at least an hour late for my inter-view. My hopes of making a good first impression were ruined. As if that weren't bad enough, I was soaking wet because I had acci-dentally left my umbrella on the last train.

Three weeks earlier, I had left New York on my grand adven-ture to London, and I was still searching for a flat. None of the landlords I had met wanted to rent to an unemployed young American. I quickly realized that decent housing, even if I could find it, was going to be a lot more expensive than I had thought. Actually, everything was a lot more expensive than I had thought. I was twenty-one and this was the first time in my life I had had to support myself. It wasn't easy. I was living out of my lightly packed suitcase in a small room at a youth hostel. The price was right, but it made my college dorm room look like a suite at the Ritz. My credit card was almost to the limit and I was running low on cash, so I was counting on this interview to get me back in the black.

I paced back and forth on the platform, trying to calm down. My stomach started to growl, reminding me that I had skipped breakfast. I reached into my pocket for some money to buy a snack, but I was shocked to find it was empty. I had had the equivalent of $100 in cash in that pocket, which was all I had left until I could get a paycheck. I searched the rest of my pockets and all through my bag, but I still couldn't find any money. In my mind, I retraced the route I had taken that morning, and remembered that in Paddington station a disheveled young man had bumped into me on the crowded platform. He ran off, and I naively thought that he was just very rude and in a big hurry. Now I realized that he was a pickpocket.

What next? I was hungry, wet, miserable, and now broke, and I had to trudge back through the rain only to spend another night in that grimy hostel. All this, and I was still no closer to finding a job. I cupped my hands over my face, sat down on the bench, and tried very hard not to cry. I was a failure at that, too.

A few minutes later, I felt someone sit down next to me. I looked up sideways into the round face of an old woman. She was very plump and hardy, and she wore a red bandanna in her hair. Her faded blue cotton dress was well worn and frayed at the hem, and her shoes desperately needed repair. Her strong hands gave away many years of hard work and struggle, but her smile was serene and easy.

"There, there, child," she said in the kind of soft Southern accent you could listen to all day. How wonderful to finally hear something familiar in this strange new city! She smiled at me and gently placed a damp piece of paper into my hand. I looked down at it and saw that it said "Jesus Loves You" in plain lettering. That was all it said.

"Now don't you forget that," the old woman said. "Jesus loves you, honey, and His love is always with you, right by your side."

She gave my hand a reassuring squeeze and quietly walked across the platform, laboring a little in her worn old shoes.

Like the flip of a switch, she had given me the certainty, despite all my frustration, that everything would work out just fine. I wiped my wet face with my coat sleeve and ran over to the stairs to thank her. But when I looked down the stairway and all around the station, I could not find her anywhere. It was as if she had just disappeared into the soggy city backdrop.

I sat down on the bench again and started wondering why that old woman came up onto the platform but didn't stay to catch the train. I also thought that it was a strange coincidence for me to run into a Southern American woman in the outskirts of London. But as I got back on the train, finally heading in the right direction, I thought that maybe meeting her really wasn't a coincidence at all.

I had heard it many times before that angels don't always have golden halos and white-feathered wings and that hope and love can be found in the most unexpected places. Now I know that's true. I know because when I was just out of college, cold, broke, scared, and very far away from home, God sent an angel to High Barnet station to remind me that I was loved. And even though I felt like a complete failure, I in fact had everything I needed to become a success.

No, I didn't get that job at the prestigious company. Instead, I got a better one. And just a week after I broke down in tears at the station, I moved into a fully furnished flat just a few blocks from Regent's Park. My grand adventure became exactly that, and although it wasn't perfect, I will always remember it as one of the best years of my life.

AMY LYNNE JOHNSON

THAT'S WHAT FRIENDS
ARE FOR

I climbed into the car with my friend Michele and her family for the short drive to Wickham Park in Melbourne, Florida. It was a bright sunny Fourth of July, and we were all on our way to a picnic.

When we arrived at the park, Michele, her brother David, and I all ran toward the lake for a cool swim. We joked and laughed as we swam, not paying attention to the warning signs: DO NOT SWIM BEYOND THIS POINT!

After a while I grew very tired, and I could no longer touch the bottom because now I was in deep water. I flipped on my back and floated for a long time, trying to regain my strength, then gradually work my way back to shore. When I finally lifted my head and began to tread water, I realized to my horror that I had floated out into the middle of the lake, far away from anyone else.

Long strands of plants wrapped around my legs as I treaded water, and my heart pounded in my ears as I realized that I could not free myself. My arms and legs ached from the strain as I struggled. I went under and swallowed water. I coughed and gasped for air. Panic gripped me as I yelled for help as loudly as I could. I looked over at Michele, who was much closer to shore than I was. She began to swim toward the shore quickly, and I thought she had not heard me.

I went under the water again, and it occurred to me that I was going to die here on this beautiful Fourth of July. My life began to pass before my eyes, and I saw everything that I had ever done. I saw my mother and wondered if she would be all right after I died. I longed to tell her I loved her just one more time. As I struggled, I prayed to God that I would live. I was only thirteen and had barely tasted life.

I didn't feel the strong arms that pulled me out of the lake until we got to shore. A young man stood over me. His face was pale. He was shaking me and asking if I was okay. I spat up a lot of water, and my breathing was labored, but finally I nodded to him, unable to speak. I looked over at Michele; she was pale too. She looked much older than her thirteen years, and suddenly I realized why she swam away from me—she had gone to get the lifeguard. Michele had saved my life.

I tried to stand up to walk, but my legs were shaking so badly I could only stumble a few feet to the shade of a tree. I sat down again still coughing violently, thanking God that I was alive. Michele sat next to me in silent shock.

At that moment, I felt changed forever. Suddenly in awe of how beautiful and wondrous life is, I knew I'd never take it for granted. Life is a precious, delicate miracle that can slip away in a heartbeat—unless you get a second chance. By having a near miss, I learned in an instant that I'm not invincible at all. Gratefully, I looked over at Michele again and knew this experience is just what friends are for.

DAWN KREISELMAN

FIRSTHAND LEARNING

*P**lato once said, "Be kind, for everyone you meet is* fighting a harder battle." Last summer, I discovered how true that is.

I felt honored to be selected to attend a week long governor's conference to learn how to incorporate a service project into my community, yet it was the first time I'd be away from family and friends. I stayed in a dorm room on the Augsburg College campus along with other high school students.

One of the main events of the week was to visit homeless shelters. My group of ten would be going to the House of Charity in downtown Minneapolis. This would be a first for me, since I came from a small, rural town in Minnesota where homelessness does not exist.

When we arrived, we went inside and sat down at one of the cafeteria tables and listened to the manager give us a brief history of the House of Charity. After she was done speaking, a man who was involved in a program that the shelter offers asked if he could tell us his story of struggle.

I remember listening to him and thinking, *This man is trying so hard to get his life back, his own life that he has lost. And he has so much determination to make of it what he can.* After he finished, I was firmly convinced that he was the best speaker I had heard all week, even better than the ones who were paid to speak to us at the convention. I suppose experience is a hard lesson, but the best teacher.

Next, the manager showed us around the small building and

told us of the opportunities for the unfortunate ones that come for help to the House of Charity. I was amazed at how hard she worked to give these people another chance at life.

When the tour was over, she asked us to stay for lunch with the homeless people, who were already getting in line to eat. We joined in, single file behind them, and suddenly this overwhelming surge of emotions gushed over me. Tears started to stream down my face as I watched people much less fortunate than me go through the line and get their food. People knowing they had to depend on others for survival. Eating food that they weren't able to pay for on their own. And here I was in name-brand clothes, healthy and happy with oh so many more blessings than these people have ever had.

What is wrong with this picture? How come I am so lucky? Why am I so blessed? Why is life so good to me and so cruel to another? How is it that today I am at this homeless shelter and tomorrow will be attending a ceremony at the governor's mansion? Experiencing two completely different worlds within a matter of two days!

All through the meal, I sat and sobbed while I ate, heaving loudly. A homeless man started talking to me, and he acted so happy. He didn't have anything, but he was smiling and taking the most out of life that he could grasp. He had so much courage, taking one step at a time, one day at a time, one meal at a time.

Halfway through lunch, the head cook stepped over to our table and asked if I was all right. With tears in my eyes, I said yes, but obviously he didn't believe me. After we finished eating, we went to a waiting area for the bus to come pick us back up. One of my counselors walked up to me and gave me a hug. I noticed there were tears in her eyes, too. So of course, I started to cry harder, with loud sobs. I was unable to control my emotions, which is very unlike me, considering I don't like to cry, especially in front of people. We had to wait about ten minutes before the bus came, and I never stopped bawling.

Before we left, the head cook came up to me again and asked if I was going to come back. I looked straight into his eyes, as mine watered up again and said, "Of course I am." He smiled at me and shook my hand as I stepped into the bus. I sat by myself the whole way back to campus, crying softly.

That night, as my roommate and I were engaged in one of our deep, nightly conversations, I told her what happened to me that day at the House of Charity. And how, for a total of about two hours, I couldn't stop crying. She turned to me, with an excited look on her face, and said, "Teresa, that was God's grace!"

Since that experience, I have realized how lucky I am for what I have and how important it is to be kind to those I know and don't know. That day at the House of Charity has been the most meaningful and powerful day of my life, and certainly my best teacher. I was moved by God's grace to use the gift He has placed in us all, enormous compassion.

TERESA ELIZABETH TRAXLER

You don't have to be afraid of change.
You don't have to worry about what's been taken away.
Just look to see what's been added.
JACKIE GREER

WISDOM AT
THE WATER'S EDGE

The summer I turned twelve had every indication of becoming the lowest point in my young life. My parents had decided to end their fifteen-year marriage. The only home I had ever known would be sold, life with my father would be reduced to a weekend experience, and I would begin seventh grade in a new school.

While all of these changes were terrifying to me that June, what disturbed me the most was forgoing our annual vacation to the mountains. Instead of spending the summer in Pennsylvania's Pocono Mountains, tucked away in the cool, verdant forest, I was going to spend the next ten weeks in New Jersey with my elderly aunt, who lived in a quiet seashore community, Avon-by-the-Sea. From what little I knew, the only friends I could expect to make were seagulls.

Needless to say, I did not want to go. I had never been a fan of gritty sand and salty surf, and though I did love my aunt, I hadn't seen her in nine years. I barely remembered her, and I sincerely doubted she would be much of a companion to me. But I had no choice in the matter. My parents were breaking up, not only with each other, but also our home. The only thing they agreed upon that summer was removing me from the battlefield.

So despite my misgivings and protests, the very day school closed, I found myself sitting on a train heading south. Beside me were two canvas bags that held my summer clothes, my books, and a daily journal I had been keeping since learning of my parents' impending divorce. Traveling with me, too, was a heart so heavy with resentment, bitterness, and loss, I found it difficult to breathe.

When the train pulled into the station, I was the last passenger to leave my seat. The conductor must have sensed how desperate I seemed, because he patted my shoulder as if to offer assurances that things would somehow sort themselves out. But I knew better, for my life would never be the same.

Waiting for me on the platform was Aunt Olivia, who was actually my grandmother's eldest sister. *Poor Olivia,* I thought. She was as much a victim as I was in this desperate situation. Her summer plans had not included a ten-week visit from a grandniece. I remember thinking how out-of-place she seemed at the station, almost like a young girl dressed up in her mother's clothes. Demure, slender, and almost shy, she smiled at me, then hesitantly patted my shoulder, in much the same manner as the conductor had. I supposed I must have looked as forlorn to her as I had to him.

Hauling my canvas bags in the direction of the taxi stand, I trudged after Aunt Olivia, who moved with surprising grace and speed for an older woman. Fortunately, the line was a short one, and Aunt Olivia and I were soon seated in an old-fashioned Checker cab heading east toward the shoreline. In no time at all, the landscape started to change. With my face pressed against the window, I noticed the city, with its traffic and people, soon receded. Within a half hour, I sensed a hint of salty air, and I viewed a series of ramshackle bungalows bearing signs like Bait and Tackle, The Chowder Shack, and Boating Supplies.

Three blocks from the ocean, Aunt Olivia directed the driver to stop in front of a small, pink cottage. As I dragged my bags up the seashell path to the front door, I tried to swallow the lump that was forming in my throat as I thought this would be my home for the next ten weeks.

Settling in with Aunt Olivia was much easier than I had anticipated. To her credit, she respected my privacy and sensed my need to be left alone. She didn't try to distract me with useless activity or engage me in meaningless chatter. Because the cottage was so tiny, my aunt had adopted a very simple lifestyle, which as I look back, was precisely what I had needed at the time. Since the dwelling was so small, I slept in an open loft, tucked in the eaves. Every night, as I climbed the ladder to my bedroom in the stars, I felt like Heidi. But unlike my storybook heroine, I had a view of the ocean—not the mountains, which were familiar to me.

During the day, I used a rusty bicycle that had once belonged to my mother. For the first few days, I purposely avoided the ocean and beach, preferring to exhaust myself pedaling alone into the town. At the time, I didn't think that much about it, but in retrospect, I think there was so much anger in me that I was unable to even see, much less appreciate, the beauty of the shoreline.

Thoughts that were too terrifying to consider merely a week ago now claimed my full attention. What would my new school be like? Would I make any friends? Would my new home be like my old one? Would I really see my father every weekend, or would those times together be replaced by new interests—like another family?

By the fourth morning, while these thoughts continued to swirl inside my head, I somehow found myself pedaling to the beach. It was a beautiful, clear sunrise, and while I had always been partial to the mountains, the seascape before me held a unique beauty. When I arrived at the beach, it was virtually empty but for two lone silhouettes—one feeding the seagulls, the other fortifying a sand castle against the approaching tide.

I left my bike on the boardwalk and ventured toward the sea. As I walked, I studied the figure feeding the gulls. There was something vaguely familiar about the stance. A natural grace, the fluid movements, almost an affinity with the sea. Then it occurred to me: it was Aunt Olivia. Dressed in worn jeans, a faded T-shirt, and a baseball cap, she resembled a young teenager from a distance. I could not help but remember the dichotomy of seeing her in the train station, stressed, strained, and out-of-place. Here, against the backdrop of the pounding surf and the beach, she was home.

Though she did not turn toward me, she sensed my presence. "Have some bread," she said softly, handing me some crusts without taking her eyes off the pair of gulls she was feeding. As I crumbled the crusts, the sound of the gulls overhead, the scent of the salty air, and the sight of the young boy defending his sand castle effected a calmness within me. I had not felt such peace since learning of my parents' impending divorce. Worries about getting acquainted with a new school, making new friends, and finding my place in a world that no longer included the only home that I had ever known were cast aside. I suddenly felt freer, lighter, like the first warm day of the year when I discarded my winter coat.

Long after the last of the bread was gone, Aunt Olivia and I continued to watch the boy. Finally, she spoke, "You have to admire the persistence in that boy," she said softly. "He's trying so hard to defend that castle. He's decorated it with beautiful shells; he's put his heart and soul into that project. But no matter how high the walls or how deep the moat he builds, the ocean is stronger and more powerful."

As she spoke, I watched the boy. The closer the tide came, the more frenzied he became. His digging became manic; his face was marked with apprehension at each wave. Finally, Aunt Olivia extended her hand to me, and together, we walked down to the water's edge.

The boy looked up at us. At first, he seemed confused, but then

I saw him smile. Aunt Olivia must have extended her other hand because the boy left his sand castle, stood up, and took her hand. As the three of us watched, a final wave crashed upon the castle, leveling it to the sand, destroying the walls, and flooding the moat.

As the seashells that had decorated the castle were scattered, Aunt Olivia released our hands. "Let's collect as many of these beautiful shells as we can," she said. "These shells were actually the best part of that castle. Let's gather them together. We'll use them to build a new castle in a more protected area." And that's just what we did.

Aunt Olivia's words would guide me on more occasions than I care to remember. That day on the beach would help me countless times, as I fought to rebuild my life after forces beyond my control sent me into a tailspin.

That fall, I began a new life when I joined my mother in a house that would soon become home. I made new friends, wonderful ones, in a new school that would offer me more academically than my old one ever could. And perhaps most important, I forged a new relationship with my parents, which included both of them in my life separately, but just as dearly as before.

BARBARA DAVEY

everal years ago, my grandmother's heart stopped beating. She had been through her second bypass heart surgery and was in intensive care, trying to recover from the trauma her body had just gone through. My grandmother's eight children and their families were staying in a nearby hotel for the duration of her recuperation. I was shadowed from much of the truth during that time, but I heard my mother talking to my father outside of the hotel room one night, "Not good . . . swelling . . . the blood, just . . . too thin . . . won't . . . stop." These words alarmed and puzzled me, left hanging over my head, not connected concretely to any sentence, yet making a statement all their own.

When my mother told me my grandmother had died, I finally understood the definition of the word "grief." A whirl of anger, fear, and disbelief consumed me as all the strength I had been relying on through the ordeal left me. The surgery that was to prevent her dying had killed her. I wept nonstop from the moment my mother told me until days later, when I was empty of tears.

At the funeral, my body could not produce the energy it would take to shed tears and I felt light, as if my spirit had left me to save itself from despair. As the priest went through the ceremony, I leaned against my mother, as helpless then as I was as an infant. The mass ended and people began to gather in line to pay their last respects to my grandmother, who lay still in her beautiful coffin.

As I sat in the pew waiting for my row to rise, I noticed a gift bag sitting on the pew before me. "What's this?" I asked my aunt. She adjusted the contents of the bag and brought out a card my five-year-old cousin, Caitlyn, had drawn. "They're gifts for Grandma," Caitlyn said as she showed me the cards. My heart tore inside as I looked at my cousin. I had nothing to offer my grandmother. I wanted to have that connection with her, to know something of mine was with her and would be with her always. I could have written her a new poem, or given her one of the many she had already inspired. Nothing, I had nothing. Tears slowly formed and began to drip down my cheeks again. I pressed my hand to my heart, surprised that it actually was aching, and felt my gold chain under my fingers. I fiddled with the charms on it as I tried to figure out what I could leave my grandmother. I rolled the little heart charm in my fingers and suddenly realized that I could give that to her.

I had found the small gold heart in my mother's jewelry box one day and asked her for it. It was a tiny thing; she could not even remember where it had come from. I connected that little heart with my own and decided to place it with my grandmother to keep with her always. My shaking fingers struggled with the latch on the chain as I walked down the pew to give it to her. I stumbled a bit, and my necklace fell out of my hands and onto the floor. I picked up the necklace, but the heart was gone from it. I turned to my mother, sobbing hard again. "Mom, my heart! It's gone. . . . Help me, please! I dropped it. I have to give it to her!"

My family searched the floor and pews for it until Caitlyn found it and gave it to me. I walked up to my grandmother, kissed the tiny heart to my lips, and laid it down next to her. The next day, my mother, her sisters and I gathered at my grandparent's house to remove my grandmother's things for my grandfather. As we sorted her things, I picked up her jewelry box and began to look through it as I always had when I visited.

My grandmother always had the cutest trinkets in her jewelry box. They were often little toys her grandchildren had given to her and she kept as treasures among her real valuables. I dropped the contents onto the bedspread and rummaged through them idly. At the bottom of the pile of her jewelry, I found a tiny charm. It was a small gold heart, the exact same kind I had taken off my necklace and given to her. "Mom, my heart! The same one she has!" My mother looked at me, tears filling her eyes as she saw the tiny shape on my fingertip.

That little heart dangles on my gold necklace to this day. I do not know where either of those little hearts came from, but I do know how important they ended up being to me. I see them as a blessing. I think it was a sign from my grandmother to move on, but to remember that as my heart will always be with hers, hers shall be with mine.

MELISSA SANDY VELA

ven if I didn't have a dream, I always had a plan. In college, I learned to be responsible and organized and to set goals that I could attain. Then everything changed. I'll never forget my finals week from college last year. Days away from graduation and miles away from home, I was diagnosed with a brain tumor. I left the hospital alone, in devastation. Unsure of what my future would hold, I shed countless tears. Although close friends eased the pain, I could not hide from my fear of facing death. Somehow, I managed to complete the exams in spite of my jangled nerves.

I began to feel different from everyone else, since my friends were graduating, celebrating, and eager to move on to new chapters in their lives. I especially found it interesting to see how others around me dealt with my news. Some acted suddenly distant for lack of words, some dramatized the whole thing, and some acted perfectly normal, which felt the most comfortable for me.

Within days, I had packed up all of my college belongings and headed home with my family ready to face this unexpected hurdle. I immediately turned to my best friend from high school. She had gone through cancer in our senior year, and because of watching her courageously overcome so many obstacles four years before, I knew she could give me the fuel I needed for my own battle.

As my surgery date to remove the tumor got closer, I was experiencing intense physical pain. Part of me wanted it over with and the other part of me was coming unglued. The wall of strength I had built was crumbling. I was so angry that I had to go through this when all those around me were going on with their lives. I spent a lot of time asking, *Why me?*

But something wonderful started happening in the midst of all this. I began to see all the beauty around me in a whole new way. The smallest things started to catch my eye. I noticed how colorful and serene a sunset could be when you took time to enjoy it. Blades of grass cascading along hillsides looked a brighter shade of green. A small child's laughter became an instant remedy for a bad day.

Miraculously, I woke up from surgery grateful to be alive and well. Words cannot describe the happiness I felt at that special moment—to be given a second chance.

My recovery was a long process as I learned to walk again and do simple tasks. I remember when I went home and studied my bald head for the first time. It shouldn't have surprised me, but it did! Ironically, a month before I knew I had a tumor, I cut my long hair short and donated it to the American Cancer Society. I discovered there's a huge difference between short and bald!

Life can sure throw a good curve ball when you least expect it. Yet I've had this new start, and I'm enjoying every minute of it. I used to hear people say you should dream the unimaginable, and I always preferred to plan instead. Now, dreaming big and following my heart's desire without knowing how it will end up is the *only* thing I have time to do.

MELISSA S. HARTMAN

VII
SORTING AND SIFTING
WITH
MOM AND DAD

The shortest distance between two points is under construction.

NOELIE ALITO

*M*y *father walked out the front door of our Allen-*town, Pennsylvania, home on a cold and drizzly Thursday morning in November of 1969. With all the inherent rights and privileges assigned to corporate vice presidents, he boarded the corporate Learjet with his peers and headed for a meeting in Wisconsin. Dense fog prevented the continuation of the flight, so the crew landed midway to wait it out. In what proved to be tragically flawed judgment, the pilot decided to continue the journey, and upon landing, he missed the runway and crashed into Lake Michigan, instantly killing all seven passengers aboard and himself. Seven women became widowed and twenty-one children became orphaned in a split second.

That loss hit me again—this time like a ton of bricks—when I hung my clothing into my tiny dorm-room closet. I noticed that my wardrobe bore little resemblance to that of my freshman roommate. Southern belle she was, coming from an old-line Charlotte family, with blood that ran blue and thick. She had better-quality clothing and much more of it.

If only Dad were still alive, I thought, *we would be much better off, and I could be more like her.*

It wasn't only my materialistic cravings, common as they were for any eighteen-year-old, that drove these feelings. It was also an all-consuming loneliness, an alienation, that now filled every pore of my being, starting with the moment I was dropped off at this very Southern, very private college I had chosen. Known for its premed program and its strong academic standards, it appealed strongly to me, a half-orphaned Northern transplant.

It was at Wake Forest University in Winston-Salem, North Carolina, where I missed my father the most. Here all girls, if they were from the South anyway, called their fathers Daddy. It was an unabashedly common and affectionate name that none of my friends up North had used since they were perhaps six or seven years old. We always referred to our father as Dad or even Father, but not here. And not only were these dads Daddy, they were frequently also referred to as Sugar Daddies.

In the South, fathers and daughters relate differently to each other than they do in the North. There is this sweet and generous bond that they have that is unlike any I had observed growing up in the North. There is a sense that Daddy can do no wrong. He'll always be there to encourage you, support you, stand up for you, and guide you. Daddy will always be there to talk you through crucial life decisions, like which boys are good enough to date, which job interviews make sense for you to spend valuable time and energy on, and which of life's frustrations are worth losing a night's sleep over and which ones aren't.

Maybe if I had stayed in the North to go to school, the absence would have seemed less profound. My mom was there for me in every way that she could have been. But she was a mom—a Northern mom. She was not and could never be a Southern Sugar Daddy.

Nonetheless, time at college taught me to be grateful for what I did have, just as it taught me that every family has its challenges. One of my dorm mates lost her father, the quintessential Southern Sugar Daddy, to a massive and sudden heart attack. Of course the news was devastating, but because I'd been through my own father's death, I felt that I could help her survive. During the course of living among other girls from all walks of life and circumstances, I discovered life hands each of us a bag of mixed blessings.

I graduated with honors, eventually earning an MBA. And in the process, I developed qualities that have served me well. If given the choice, of course, I would prefer to be a loving daughter of a loving and very much alive Daddy. But that wasn't God's plan. The void still exists for me without my dad, but I've come to be grateful anyway for how my tenacious and resilient spirit has prevailed.

CAROLINA FERNANDEZ

A mother is not a person to lean on
but a person to make leaning unnecessary.
Dorothy Canfield Fisher

A MIND OF MY OWN

I told myself that Robert had made a foolish mistake when he broke up with me. Oh, I knew about Mary and two other girls, but I just didn't think it was over between us. I truly believed I could change his mind. And his heart.

There were two weddings on June 17. My sister-in-law Marilu was matron of honor for her brother Bill and his bride-to-be Melanie. Marilu and Bill's family always hosted fun weddings, and all of us loved an excuse to party. But Robert's big brother was getting married the same day. Since Robert and I had dated for nearly two years, I knew Jack and the bride-to-be, Margaret well.

I was determined to go to Jack and Margaret's wedding. The romantic atmosphere would be perfect to get Robert back as my steady boyfriend.

"Why do you want to go to *that* wedding?" my mother had asked me when I told her my plans.

"I was invited. It's what I want to do," I told her.

"But what about Bill and Melanie?"

"Mom, it's no big deal. With so many guests around, no one will miss me."

"How will you get there? We're all going to Bill and Melanie's wedding."

"It's easy, Mom. Jack and Margaret's wedding is at the university. Bill and Melanie's wedding is at Fort Sam Houston. The two places are barely a mile from each other." I had gone over everything in my mind, so I had all the right answers.

My mother shrugged and walked away to check that my sister and my three little brothers were dressing appropriately for a wedding. I was relieved to be part of a big family because I could slip away and no one would notice.

Since Marilu was so involved with Bill's wedding, her husband (my big brother) Gilbert, was volunteered to drive me to the university, where Jack and Margaret's wedding mass was being held.

While he didn't question my mother's request to give me a ride down the road, he asked me as we drove along why I was going.

"Why not? They invited me." I gave him a good answer, I thought.

He nodded. I felt so proud of myself. Everything was happening exactly as I had planned.

Gilbert told me he'd return at five o'clock, as he dropped me off in front of the university chapel.

I entered the chapel just as the wedding ceremony began. I quietly found a spot on the groom's side of the church. Immediately, I looked in the front pews for Robert. He was seated with his parents, trying to keep Emily, his five-year-old niece, from running off. His eldest sister and her husband sat on the other side.

The wedding ceremony was sweet and charming. I remembered when Robert and I had attended Gilbert and Marilu's wedding together. The wedding had made us both feel so romantic. Later at the reception when we danced together, I had told Robert that even though we were only sixteen, I knew we were meant for each other. On that day, he kept kissing me and agreed with everything I said.

That's why I knew I had done the right thing by coming to this wedding. And when Robert saw me today, I knew he was going to agree with me again.

I waited until the ceremony was over and the bridal party had assembled at the chapel altar for pictures. Then I made my presence known. The first people I greeted were Jack and Margaret. They were hugging everybody and looked happy to see me.

I turned to Robert's parents next. They responded to my greetings with raised eyebrows and nervous smiles. I told myself they were glad to see me too; they were probably anxious from all the wedding activities.

I shook hands with Robert's oldest sister and her husband and waved at little Emily, who gave me a wonderful smile.

I felt so excited when Robert and I finally made eye contact. But instead of welcoming me, he turned away and walked out a side door.

I decided that he wanted to avoid all the people at the front door of the church. He had always been shy among a crowd of strangers.

I followed other guests to the next building for the wedding reception. I went to the ladies' room first to check myself out. I had worn Robert's favorite dress. My long hair was curly and shiny, just the way he liked it.

Finally I found him sitting alone near the windows overlooking the balcony. I knew he had chosen the romantic spot just for us. I gave him a winner's smile. A smile that I knew would change his mind about us.

"What are you doing here, Diane?" he asked me.

I had an answer ready. "I was invited. Remember how we planned to come to the wedding together?"

"That was before we broke up. What if I had brought another girl?"

"But you didn't. And I'm here. Aren't you glad I came?"

He didn't look glad at all. There was no love reflected in those blue-gray eyes that I admired. He just sat in a chair, his lips pressed together in a straight line. He made me feel like an uninvited, unwanted guest.

I couldn't fool myself any longer.

Not only was it over between Robert and me, but also I was an outsider to this family's celebration. Why had I come? I stood in a room filled with people and had never felt so lonely.

"Could you please leave?" he said, and then he got up to stand near Jack and Margaret, who stood talking to people I didn't know.

As they all looked at me, I smiled at the wedding couple. I did a finger wave, before I walked out of the reception hall.

I sat on the steps of the university chapel and waited only fifteen minutes before Gilbert showed up in his car.

I glanced at my watch and got into the front seat with him. "You're early."

"Mom said you might be finished sooner than you thought."

I just stared out the car window, feeling sad and stupid. When I got back to Bill and Melanie's wedding, I just knew that Mom would have a big *I told you so* waiting for me.

When I walked into the other wedding reception, my big sister grabbed me by the arm and introduced me to some of Bill's handsome college friends. Dad walked over and told me he wanted a dance later. Bill's mom waved and smiled at me. So did Bill and Melanie. And my little brothers informed me that I hadn't missed the best part, the wedding cake.

Finally, I had to face my mom. She was coming toward me with a plate of finger sandwiches in her hand.

"How did it go with Robert?" she asked.

That's when I realized I hadn't fooled anyone but myself. She knew why I had gone to the other wedding. I was the one who had made a foolish mistake.

I couldn't lie to her or to myself anymore.

"It was a disaster, Mom. He didn't want me there at all."

She put down the plate of sandwiches and put her arm around

my shoulders. She squeezed me close. "This is where you belong, Diane, with your family. I'm glad you're here now. Let's go help Mrs. Little serve the wedding cake, okay?"

I realized my mom didn't have to let me go to Robert's brother's wedding, but she did. She knew I was stubborn, and that I had to make this mistake to grow up.

I had a mother who let me learn for myself that you can't force a person to love you. And at the same time, she taught me to appreciate the fact that no matter how stubborn I acted, Mom would always love me.

I hope I can be that wise when my daughter grows a mind of her own too.

DIANE GONZALES BERTRAND

MELTING ICE

January 4, 2000

There are nine pieces of crumpled paper lying around me on my desk right now. Each paper is covered in scribbled, scratched-out, rejected words. They are words that don't fit. I can't make them fit, and it's frustrating me. All I am trying to do is write a simple letter. How hard can it be? One letter. That's all. Why can I never complete this one task that feels so important?

January 15

Deep breath in . . . 2 . . . 3 . . . 4 . . . out . . . 2 . . . 3 . . . 4. I think I have finished. I think I may have actually finally finished my letter to my father. It turned out so short. So simple, to the point . . . so formal and so unlike me. That's how I said I wanted it. Just wanted to get my point across. Didn't want him to be able to read anything into it. Lord, this is scary. What if I actually send it? What then? My math teacher, Mr. Lynch, would say the ball is in his court now. I gave him the choice; he must make the move. My part is played. Dear God, this is scary.

January 21

I recopied my letter today. Thought about asking my mom for his address. Not yet. Give it a few days. I have to make sure this is the right thing. I don't want to make a mistake here. Not with him.

I was thinking about him today. Thinking about the handful of memories I still have of him. It's rather pitiful; I can count them on one hand. They're not all pretty memories, either. I suppose that's expected, though, when you have a father who left when you were still in your crib and hasn't visited you in over a decade.

He called once. I was in sixth grade and fatefully answered the telephone that night. I still remember that phone call. This man whom I hadn't heard from in years was suddenly gushing out how much he loved me. He called me honey-pooh. "This is Daddy, honey-pooh," he said. I wanted to puke. Wanted to scream at him that he was not my daddy and never would be; wanted to shriek out that he gave up that responsibility when he left me and my brother Colin. I swallowed my words, though, and handed the phone to my mom. The only reason he called was that the government was finally hounding him for the child support money he had never paid. He wanted my mom to get them off his back. Figures. The man only calls when he wants something.

These are the thoughts that make me never want to send that letter. Even so, I need to put an end to the phantom my father has become. I gave him two choices: write me back if he wants to know who I am and is willing to tell me a little bit about who he is, or ignore my letter completely and end it there. If need be, I can slam the door in his face with a satisfying "bang." If he does write back . . . well, I guess I'll just have to see what comes of this mess.

January 22

Phew, I thought writing the letter would be the toughest part of all this. I was wrong. Tonight I had to get my father's address from my mom.

I made it home by my curfew this evening. Right on time. My mom was in a pleasant mood, casually watching TV. The house was quiet; everyone else had already gone to bed. The moment I walked in, I knew tonight had to be it. I tromped into my room, grabbed the envelope with that solitary name in its center, and forced my feet back toward the living room. A few steps away, I froze. I guess now I know what it's like to have your feet turn into lead. I couldn't move.

Finally, I swallowed hard, bit my lip, and just pushed myself through the doorway, brilliantly blowing my own cover, completely against my better judgment. It was too late to turn back. Mom had seen me and knew something was up. So I walked in, quietly cursing myself, laid the envelope down in front of her, and asked softly, "Do you have his address?"

God bless my mom. She always knows just what to say and how to say it. As we talked, mother and daughter, heart to heart, I could see the pieces of this crazy puzzle my of life beginning to fit together and it felt good. Really good. Maybe everything will work out. Who knows? All I know is that I am ready to move forward now.

January 26

I thought this last step would be more difficult. But my knees held strong and my hands remained steady as I slipped the thin white envelope quietly into the big, blue gaping mailbox in front of my local post office. Maybe this won't turn out so bad after all. I feel I'm prepared for anything now. Bring on the dogs, I shall stand tall. I know who I am, and whatever happens, my foundation will not be shaken. Lord, guide that letter to the hands of the one it is meant for. His silence, his rejection, his sugary sappiness, his anger, or his love . . . Now is my time. I am ready to face it all.

BRIANNA MAHIN-AYERS

One is not born a woman, one becomes one.
SIMONE DE BEAUVOIR

A RITE OF PASSAGE

I was twelve years old when I got my first period, the blessing from God, the breaking into womanhood, the source of all wisdom—or so I thought.

Some people cried when they got "it" for the first time, but not me. I had been waiting for my period for as long as I could remember. That afternoon, my prayers had been answered, and all my patience had paid off. I was ecstatic, as if I just asked Matthew Wilson, the most popular boy in our homeroom, out to the movies and he said, "Yes, I would love to."

Finally, my bragging rights would be granted. I could now voice my opinions at those sophisticated group meetings Lena, the eldest of our sixth-grade class, would lead. Lena started her period first last April, which made her the expert among my girlfriends on almost any topic. We would listen carefully to whatever Lena said then apply it to our lives. But those intense conversations didn't tell me what to expect when my period came, and my mother certainly never talked about what happens when puberty hits.

Once, Mom and I were in a clothing store, and as if she was talking to the air instead of me, she said, "You know, I should buy this type of underwear just in case you get your period." My mother's conversation was as awkward and uncomfortable as riding a bike with a pad on, as I would soon find out.

The afternoon I got my period was indeed cause for celebration. A rite of passage. A don't-forget-to-write-this-down-in-your-journal day. I was having my first period and I thought nothing could ruin it, nothing could go wrong, nothing . . . until I told my mother.

That afternoon, a few minutes after I got home from school, I sat on the toilet. I inhaled my soon-to-be-adult life then slowly exhaled my childhood. I could not wait to tell the good news to my mother, who was downstairs doing her weekly loads of laundry.

I was a woman now, a big girl, and could have babies. I leaned over the bathroom sink with both hands pressed palms down on the counter and looked into the mirror. My braided hair extensions hung down long in front and against the sides of my face. I pulled my braids back into a ponytail. Maybe I was becoming the spitting image of my mother, as everyone said. My dark brown eyes, my chocolate-smooth skin, the round shape of my head, and my thin, stern lips all belonged to her. If I was the epitome of my mother, why was I so distant from her? *Perhaps,* I thought, *today would finally make a difference.* I smiled at my reflection, let my hair down again, and hurried downstairs to tell Mom.

The laundry door was closed, so I gently opened it. Mom looked tired. She was putting the colors into the washing machine.

"Mum, I got my period," I said grinning.

She looked at me for a brief moment and resumed sorting the laundry.

"Do you know how to put a pad on?" she asked, not looking up.

"Yes," I answered. I stood there.

It was all over that very moment. My smile faded. It was as if the excitement I had felt in the bathroom had been yanked from my body, strangled, and left alone to die on the laundry room floor. She said nothing about becoming a woman, nothing about all the myths passed down from generation to generation, and certainly nothing about babies. I left the laundry room with tears in my eyes and an empty page in my journal.

Eight years later, at the age of twenty, I still haven't told my mother that story. For a long time, I silently blamed her for anything that went wrong in my life, until one summer afternoon coming back from the hair salon.

Mother was in the driver's seat, and we were stopped at a red light, giving my mom time to admire her reflection and newly styled hairdo in the rearview mirror. As she looked at herself, I looked at her from the corner of my eye. Suddenly, she stopped touching her hair and said, "Every time I look at my face," she paused a little, "I can still see my mother." She pushed the visor back up, wiped a tear from her eye, and looked straight ahead. With that, I realized that my mother was human. She rarely talked about her past, and she never talked about her mother with such emotion. Her mother had died when Mom was just fifteen. With newfound compassion for all my mom had gone through as a teen without a mom, I silently forgave her for whatever she did or didn't do the day my period started.

Now when I kiss Mom hello or goodbye, I do it with sincerity instead of out of obligation. Our conversations are warmer, and I'm interested in what she has to say. And I'm eternally grateful for this woman who gave me life.

Today when I look in the mirror, I see my mother looking right back at me. I cannot help but think that I am indeed blessed for the relationship Mom and I are building—now and forever.

My first period was over quickly. My true rite of passage happened later—when I acquired wisdom and compassion, necessary qualities to "pass go" and rightfully cross over into womanhood.

JOELLE YANICK JEAN

DADDY'S LITTLE GIRL

"Please, Daddy," I said. "All the other girls in my class have pierced ears."

"I'm sorry, honey," Daddy said. "You can't get your ears pierced until you are sixteen." I didn't think that I could wait until I turned sixteen. I was almost the only girl in my class that wasn't showing off her dangling earrings to all of her friends. All the boys smiled when they saw the beautiful, grown-up jewelry those girls wore.

Sixteen must be a magical year, I thought. I understood why everyone referred to the age of sixteen as "sweet." That was the year that Daddy said I could start dating. He had already said that I could stay out until eleven o'clock—but not until after my sixteenth birthday, of course. At only twelve years of age, sixteen seemed like a million years away.

My thirteenth birthday was quickly approaching. *Now's the time to ask Daddy about my ears again,* I thought. Surely when I become a teenager he will change his mind. I began trying to convince my mom that I really needed my ears pierced. *Maybe she can talk some sense into him.* She didn't comment when I discussed it with her. I know that she went to bat for me, but Daddy was determined to disallow it until that magical sixteenth year.

My mom gave me a beautiful pair of earrings for my birthday. They looked like pierced earrings, but they weren't. They were the stick-on kind. They were precious tiny ladybugs. *At least I can fool all the kids at school,* I thought. The next day, I got all dressed up in a beautiful red dress and carefully stuck my earrings in the center of my earlobes. I felt so beautiful, just like all the other girls in my class.

Each time that I passed a mirror, I stopped to admire my ladybugs. My new earrings were the topic of conversation that day. I felt so special and grown-up.

When I returned home that day, I looked in the mirror in the living room to get another look at my precious earrings. The right one was missing! I was heartbroken. I looked all around the house. When I couldn't find it there, I tracked my path back to school. For hours I searched for the missing earring. By the time Daddy got home, I was in tears. I knew that I would have to admit to all of my friends that my ears weren't pierced after all.

When Daddy came in, he saw me crying.

"What's wrong, honey?" he asked.

"I lost my earring," I said. I heard my mother mumble something under her breath.

The next morning, Daddy got up early to go to work. He came into my room and kissed me goodbye but didn't say anything. When I got up to get ready for school, my heart was heavy. I was so sad that my cute earring had disappeared.

When I went to the breakfast table, my mother smiled. "Guess what?" she said. "We're going to get your ears pierced Saturday."

"But what about Daddy?" I asked.

"When he saw how sad you were over the lost earring and realized the effort you put forward to finding it, he agreed that you are mature enough at thirteen to get your ears pierced," she said.

The next Saturday, we got up early and went to have my ears pierced.

"You sure are pretty," Daddy said, when he saw my new earrings. "But you are growing up entirely too fast." He handed me a tiny box. I smiled when I opened it and saw two tiny ladybugs tucked away in the box. This time they were real pierced earrings, not the stick-on type, which were easy to lose.

"Can I start dating now?" I asked Daddy.

"Not on your life," he demanded. "Not until you're sixteen. Unfortunately honey, you'll be sixteen too soon," he said. We hugged each other. As we parted, I saw a tear on Daddy's cheek. I realized that this wasn't really about earrings and dates. It was about a man trying to keep his little girl from growing up too quickly. In spite of his efforts, however, my sweet sixteenth birthday arrived too soon.

"It's all happening too fast," he whispered from time to time. "You'll always be Daddy's little girl." And he was right. I never outgrew my need for my father, regardless of the earrings or the dates. He was and will always be a very special man in my life.

NANCY B. GIBBS

When there is love, there is no tiring.
AMMACHI

A WHOLE NEW PERSPECTIVE

I *was fourteen at the time of my mom's diagnosis with* cancer. It hit hard and fast. All of a sudden, my life was thrown into a whirlwind of the unknown. My mom was sitting across from me with tears rolling down her face like a fast drip in the faucet. My dad was speechless, and he quickly left the room. My younger brother Keaton and I just sat motionless, eyes wet and lips trembling.

"Cancer," my mom said, "I have cancer." The tears puddled up even more and spilled over.

What is cancer? What does that mean? My immediate thought was that she was going to die. My grandma had just died one year before from breast cancer. I never knew much about cancer, but I did know that thousands of people died from it and my mom could be next.

At first I spent all my school hours thinking about my mom and all my nonschool hours sitting by her hospital bed watching her fade in and out of sleep. Sometimes she looked at me directly and sometimes she seemed lost in her own world. Many afternoons I would sit at the end of her bed, and we both would gaze out the window, thinking in silence.

Everything took a twist as soon as my mom left the hospital. It was almost like the disease had entered not only our family but also our home. I always believed that when people left the hospital they were fine. I was proven wrong. My mom left the hospital sick and came home sick.

Before her illness, we were a very distant family, living our own lives. Sometimes you wouldn't even know we were related. We would go to our separate rooms, talk on separate phone lines, and watch separate TV shows.

This all changed the day my mom got cancer. It was as if we were thrown into a clothes dryer, tumbled around together, and then told to walk the straight line together. I believe God has a purpose for everything, and I feel He had a plan for us.

My mom used to do a lot of work around the house, but all of a sudden she was not able to. The rest of us had to learn how to work together and get the chores done. I had to take over some of Mom's role. I got up early in the morning, fixed breakfast, woke my brother Keaton up, took care of the animals, cooked dinner, helped Dad, and took care of Mom.

During my mom's emotional journey, I learned a lot. I became very responsible. There were no questions asked. I just did what I had to do, and I learned to juggle many things at once.

On this path, I also learned a lot about relationships with people, especially with my mom. We weren't all that close before her cancer, not close enough to sit down and share what was in our souls. Somewhere in the middle of all this, I became very close with her. I used to think that it wasn't cool to talk with my parents. Not now!

Every day I would go into her room and sit by her side. Many times we wouldn't say a word for hours, and some other days we would talk for hours. No matter what the day was like, we could always feel each other's presence. The way our relationship grew reminded me of a rose that is about to bloom. It opens one petal at a time, and once it opens, the beauty is magnificent.

Later on, my mom's journey became less intense and my journey started to speed up. I had become so close to my family that it became easier to relate to them than to my friends. Knowing that it was hard for my friends to understand what I'd been through and hard for me to describe it, I used writing as a form of healing all the emotions I'd been feeling. Every night I would embrace my teddy bear while letting the pen roll my thoughts onto paper. I was able to release all my fears onto the page. Since the writing was a release, I didn't keep much of it. After a year, I stopped writing every night and slowly my anxiety and Mom's cancer disappeared.

Even though this experience has slipped out of my everyday thoughts, it didn't slip out of my life. Now that I know that I can really *be there* for my family in times of need, my mom's cancer has changed my perspective forever—for the good.

DANA MASSIE

I *hesitate to commit these events to paper because I* probably don't know what I'm doing and my son isn't here to stop me.

When we checked our entering freshman into his new dormitory at Arizona State University, he took the occasion to point out to my husband and me—vociferously—that we just didn't know anything. On the other hand, this lad did, which makes the next four years seem superfluous, not to mention a drain on our savings. Were it not for the nocturnal extracurricular activities in which he hopes to engage, the scheduled courses would only gild the lily.

"No, Dad, my textbooks don't go on that shelf. That's where I want my stereo."

"Mom, don't put my pens in that desk drawer. I'll never find them."

"Extra towels? Why do I need extra towels? I have a perfectly good one in the bathroom."

He orchestrated our every action from the comfort of his bed.

My husband and I will try to muddle through the days to come without the benefit of our son's counsel on every topic. And maybe, with the passage of time, my facial tic will hardly be noticeable.

Our son had a male roommate and male suite mates, and from that point on, the dynamics changed. Coeds—each one more eye-catching than the one before—lived directly across the hall. Females were housed everywhere on his floor. It was a totally mixed-gender dorm. Our son was a recent graduate of an all-boys high school. He was trying hard to appear cool, with his hooded eyelids, a bored expression, and his I-can't-be-bothered attitude, but from long experience, I was familiar with every nuance of his act, and he was definitely drinking in the scenery and checking out the ladies.

That afternoon we old folks were bade a hasty goodbye. Our young man, far from needing to cling to the comfort and security of his family, was anxious to settle into his new and wonderful parent-free zone.

My husband and I treated ourselves to a dinner of steak and lobster, drowning our sorrows in melted butter. And all this delicious revenge was on a weeknight, no less. As we rattled around in the booth that was too vast for just the two of us, we discussed the events of that auspicious day. How could one textbook cost $75? Where had the years gone? How could our child suddenly be in college? Wonder when we'd ever get the hang of being parents? And what were the odds he'd spend more time studying the girls than his books?

I recalled one of the most poignant and beloved quotes attributed to Mark Twain: "When I was a boy of fourteen, my father was so ignorant I could hardly stand to have the old man around. But when I got to be twenty-one, I was astonished at how much the old man had learned in seven years."

Today I'm wallowing in the luxury of our empty nest. Our son's bed is neatly made, his room is tidy, and gone is the pong of sweaty socks and athletic shoes. The rafters no longer shudder with the steady thud of the bass turned up to full volume. I plan to spend this quiet time catching up on pasting photos in his baby book. The last eighteen years have kept me sort of busy.

And the future? Let's just say I smiled at each and every coed in the dorm. I wanted to make a good first impression in case one of the girls ever accompanied our son home to meet his mom.

LANA ROBERTSON HAYES

MORE CHOCOLATE STORIES?

Do you have a short story you want published that fits the spirit of *Chocolate for a Teen's Heart?* I am planning future editions, using a similar format, that will feature love stories, divine moments, overcoming obstacles, following our intuition, or embarrassing event and humorous stories that teach us to laugh at ourselves. I am seeking touching stories of one to four pages in length that warm our hearts and encourage us to see the bright side of everything we experience.

I invite you to join me in these future projects by sending your special true story for consideration. If your story is selected, you will be paid $100, you'll be listed as a contributing author, and a biographical paragraph about you will be included. For more information, or to send a story, please contact:

Kay Allenbaugh
P. O. Box 2165
Lake Oswego, Oregon 97035

Or visit my Web site: http://www.chocolateforwomen.com and read the sample teen stories, then email me your story.

kay@allenbaugh.com

CONTRIBUTORS

URSULA BACON fled Nazi Germany with her parents and spent the next nine years in China. She was interned, along with 18,000 other European refugees, by Japanese occupation forces in Shanghai for four years. She emigrated to the United States at the end of World War II. Ursula is married to author Thorn Bacon, and they operate a small publishing house and write books. She is the co-author of *Savage Shadows* (New Horizon, NY) and the author of *The Nervous Hostess Cookbook*, March 1996. (503) 682-9821

CAROLYN BERG is a tenth-grade student at Cabrillo High School in Lompoc, California, where she lives with her parents and four younger siblings—Patrick, Brinton, Timothy, and Brianna. She enjoys writing, reading, singing, playing musical instruments, acting, and hanging out with friends. She hopes to someday to go to college and study writing. She is a harpist of nine years and is currently working with her teacher, Ira, training for national competition in Washington, D.C. Chocoholic126@aol.com

DIANE GONZALES BERTRAND lives in San Antonio, Texas, where she is Writer-in-Residence at St. Mary's University. Her essay "A Mind of My Own" was inspired by a class discussion with her college students about foolish mistakes. She credits her mother's wisdom as a survival tool during her teenage years. She's published novels for teens, including *Sweet Fifteen, Lessons of the Game,* and *Trino's Choice.* dbertrand@stmarytx.edu

Suzanne Bertrand is a middle school student at St. Gregory's School. She was born into a family that encouraged her imagination and her creativity. She hopes to combine her love of art and her love of animals into a career as a scientist and to draw the animals she studies. She lives in San Antonio, Texas, with her parents, her brother, three Boxer dogs, and dozens of stuffed animals.

Alicia Billington is a sixteen-year-old junior in the international baccalaureate program. She enjoys cross country, track, and the beach. She plays classical music on the piano but also listens to rap in her free time. Her aspirations for the future are to attend Cornell University in Ithaca, New York, and have a major in science. Adevilgal@aol.com

Kimberly Birkland is a sophomore at Loyola Marymount University in Los Angeles, California. She's written for her college newspaper in the Arts & Entertainment section. Originally from Portland, Oregon, she interned at the *Lake Oswego Review* newspaper last summer. She hopes to receive formal writing instruction in the future. ksbirkland@aol.com

Maureen A. Bothe manages an Internet site for teen girls called Razzberry.com and writes a monthly column for MissClick.com. Her articles and stories have appeared in many online publications, including Cybergrrl.com and Moxie.ca. Her love for England and for great literature prompted her current work in progress—a novel about a strong-willed young woman set in Victorian England. She thanks God for her life; her father August for his appreciation of the arts; and her mother Mary for her continued inspiration and support. maureen@maureenbothe.com. Web site: www.maureenbothe.com

Margie Boulé is a general-interest columnist for *The Oregonian* in Portland, Oregon. The winner of numerous national and regional journalism awards, she also has performed as a singer with symphony orchestras around the country and as an actress/singer in opera, musical theater, and with the band Pink Martini. She currently performs in Portland with ComedySportz, an improvisational comedy troupe. marboule@aol.com

NICOLE DOMINIQUE BURGAN is a student at LaGuardia High School in Manhattan, where she studies acting. She enjoys the theater and has not yet decided what profession she wants to pursue when she finishes school. Her favorite thing to do is write poetry and short stories. She continues to submit different pieces of work to magazines and publishing companies and aspires to one day release her own book of poetry. Crew of five@juno.com

RENIE SZILAK BURGHARDT was born in Hungary and came to the United States in 1951 as a young refugee of World War II. As a freelance writer, she has contributed her work to *Angels on Earth, Mature Living, Cat Fancy, Midwest Living, Amateur Chef, Country America, Good Old Days, Whispers from Heaven,* and other publications. She also writes full time for the Internet. Some sites include Family Click.com, Whoodoo.com, Folks Online.com, On the Bright Side, Shouting Out.com, At the Fence.com, and a regular column called Nature Sketches on Suite 101.com She resides in the Ozarks of southern Missouri and enjoys nature, raising animals, her garden, and three young granddaughters. Renie@cinet.net

MICHELE WALLACE CAMPANELLI enjoys the part she's playing in creating a national bestselling *Chocolate* series. She lives on the space coast of Florida with her husband Louis. She is a graduate of Writer's Digest School and Keiser College. Author of *Margarita, The Case of the Numbers Kidnapper, Jamison,* and *Keeper of the Shroud,* published by Hollis Books, and *Hero of Her Heart,* published by Blue Note Books, she finds writing novels and screenplays her outlet for artistic expression. Currently she is working on *Black Widow,* a novel about the rock band. www.michelecampanelli.com

TALIA CARNER is a novelist with three yet-to-be-published novels. Her theme is motherhood threatened by big government. Before writing full-time, she founded Business Women Marketing Corporation, a consulting firm whose clients were Fortune 500 companies, and was the Publisher of *Savvy Woman* magazine. Active in women's civic and professional organizations, she teaches entrepreneurial skills to women and participated in the NGO women's conference in Beijing in 1995. She is Israeli-born and served in the army during the 1967 Six-Day War. She and her husband and four children live on Long Island, New York. TalYof@aol.com

KIM CHAMPION lives in Phoenix, Arizona with her husband Wayne and her two teenage sons, Adam and Jonathan. She writes poetry, comedy, and parody and has been writing personalized poetry for over twenty years under the name "Poetics Unlimited." She is a ventriloquist (thanks to the inspiration and kindness of Jimmy Nelson). She and her puppet, Stanley, have performed at Hospitals, Nursing homes, schools, and private parties. She someday dreams of writing a bestseller. Bergen2123@aol.com

BARBARA DAVEY is an executive director at Christ Hospital in Jersey City, New Jersey, where she is responsible for public relations and fundraising. She holds bachelor's and master's degrees in English from Seton Hall University. A service near to her heart is the Look Good, Feel Better program, which supplies complimentary wigs and cosmetics to women undergoing treatment for cancer. Her attitude toward life is "expect a miracle!" She and her husband, Reinhold Becker, live in Verona, New Jersey. wisewords2@aol.com

MICHELLE DUNN is a freelance writer and is currently working on her first novel. She and her husband are Australians but travel and work throughout the United States. paulandshelly@hotmail.com

ELLEN DURR lives in the mountains of western Maryland, where she writes and works as a training consultant. She sees the underlying theme of her work as "learning the art of applying the lessons for living we were given as little people to our adult lives." Her story, "Having Ourselves a Gentle Day," is in honor of her grandmother, Grace, who blessed loads of children with simple, wonderful, and profound lessons on their family farm in Greene County, Pennsylvania. She's currently working on a collection of Grace's wisdom. (301) 759-2552. ellendurr@prodigy.net

JILL FANCHER is fifteen years old. Her full name is Jill Joo-Mi Amanda Fancher, and she was born in Seoul, Korea. She will be attending the Burnsville High School starting this year. She enjoys playing soccer, reading, school, hanging out with her friends, and spending time with her family. Her faith has a special place in her heart. She resides in Burnsville, Minnesota. jfanch007@hotmail.com

KELSEY FEKKES is thirteen years old and lives in Ventura, California (near the ocean). She has a little brother who is five. Some of the things she likes to do are skateboard, camp, hang out with her friends, shop, swim, run, dance, draw, and travel. She went to Holland with her dad when she was eleven.

CAROLINA FERNANDEZ, M.B.A., left her job as a stockbroker with Merrill Lynch when she started her family. She now runs a home-based business marketing a line of custom-designed handpainted children's playwear that bears her name. Relying heavily on her own brood of four for much of her material, she has written her first book on creative motherhood and is active in a wide variety of writing and public speaking platforms to encourage mothers and inspire their creativity. Her strength and hope stem from a deep and abiding faith in God. She lives with her husband Ernie, and Nicolas, Benjamin, Cristina, and Victor in Ridgefield, Connecticut. (203) 894-8977. www.carolinafernandez.com

NANCY B. GIBBS is a weekly religion columnist and freelance writer. Her writing has appeared in many publications, such as *Honor Books, Guideposts Books,* and *Angels on Earth.* Her stories have also appeared in *Chocolate for a Teen's Soul* and *Chocolate for a Woman's Blessings.* She is a pastor's wife and the mother of three grown children. Daiseydood@aol.com

ALICIA WILDE HARDING lives on the Massachusetts coast with her husband and three children. As a middle school teacher, she is intimately acquainted with the adolescent psyche. She was previously published by Hysteria Publications in *Pandemonium or Life With Kids,* and *I Killed June Cleaver.* mah608hmh@aol.com

MELISSA S. HARTMAN is a designer and writer residing in Minnesota. She became motivated after her own life-threatening illness. Another contributing author, Candis Fancher, also provided Melissa with inspiration through her time of crisis. (612) 492-6172.

LANA ROBERTSON HAYES, who has an M.A. in education, is the author of many humorous essays, articles, and greeting cards. A former teacher, she wields her pen at life's absurdities, which she finds amusing, and her family's antics, which strike her as hilarious. A transplanted Southerner, she now lives in Arizona but still misses her native state of Georgia. BritishTea@aol.com

SARAH HORST is twenty years old and attending Harrisburg Community College in Lebanon, Pennsylvania. She plans on graduating sometime in 2002. She lives at home with her parents and younger brother. In her spare time she enjoys reading, writing poetry, watching movies, and listening to music. aplaceinthefrog@chickmail.com

SHEILA S. HUDSON, Bright Ideas founder, is a freelance writer, a speaker, and a wife/mother/grandmother. Her credits include stories in *Chocolate for a Teen's Soul, Chocolate for a Woman's Blessing, Chocolate for a Woman's Heart, God's Vitamin C for the Spirit of Men, Taking Education Higher, Casas por Cristo: Stories from the Border, Life's Little Rule Book,* and *From Eulogy to Joy.* She is a frequent contributor to *Christian Standard, Lookout, The Athens Magazine,* and *Athens Parent.* (706) 546-5085. sheila@naccm.org

JOELLE YANICK JEAN is twenty years old and a junior at Boston College. She is an English major and plans on going into the field of advertising or journalism. She loves singing and staying up late. One day she hopes to write a book about her life and her family. She also wants to start her own magazine. jeanjo@bc.edu

AMY LYNNE JOHNSON is a past contributor to the *Chocolate* series. She's a writer living in Sarasota, Florida, where she is currently working on books for children as well as several volunteer projects. AmyJ97209@aol.com

PAOLA JUVENAL is a writer and fiction consultant presently earning her M.F.A. in creative writing and translation at a university in the Midwest. She still takes ballet class every once in a while.

LINDA L.S. KNOUSE lives with her husband in the suburbs of Philadelphia and has been the chronicler of her family since early childhood. She gets her writing ability from her mother, whose vivid pictures of family history were often repeated in the form of storytelling. Linda is a freelance writer for Montgomery Publishing. LLKnouse@usa.net

DAWN KREISELMAN is a poet and short-story writer. She lives in Florida with her husband Ben and her children Eve and Teelah. Her hobbies include playing guitar, working out, and just having fun with her kids.

ALEXANDRA LEWIS is a freshman at Lincoln High School in Portland, Oregon. She enjoys writing stories and poems. She has publicly read several of her poems through Poet Speak, a Northwest organization that focuses on spreading the beauty of poetry. She loves spending time with her friends and family. This is her first published story. lewisr@pdx.edu

BRIDGET LOPEZ is delighted to be part of the *Chocolate* series. After over a decade in the New York hotel business, she left to go back to college, with the support and encouragement of her husband Dave. She graduated from Marymount Manhattan College this year with honors and a B.A. in English after serving as editor of the school's literary review her senior year. She is currently working as a freelance editor as she continues to write her short stories, essays, and plays.

NETTIE R. LUCIO has lived in San Antonio since birth. She married Jose S. Lucio after graduation from high school, and they have three children. She started working at St. Mary's University Academic Library in October 1977. As an evening studies student, she recently received her Bachelor of Arts in Communication Studies. nettie@stmarytx.edu

BRIANNA MAHIN-AYERS is seventeen years old and a lover of the theater, camping and the outdoors, playing the trumpet, swimming, and participating in church activities. She is a senior in high school who has fun spending time with friends and family alike. She aspires to someday become a full-time writer. For now, she bides her time with schoolwork and a part-time job. britg1@jps.net

DANA MASSIE is an adventurous individual who dedicates her life to exploring. She spent one year living in a remote mountainous village of sixty people. She was also an exchange student in Japan, and during that time, developed a great love for the Japanese culture. In addition to Japan she has traveled in the Pacific Rim and Europe, learning about new cultures. When not exploring, she is working on her own business, hand-cutting dog silhouettes out of wood. (360) 236-7293

CAROLINE MILLESON is a freshman at Lincoln High School in Portland, Oregon. She loves to coach soccer on those crisp and clear mornings, and to play year round with her school and private clubs. She lives with her parents, sister, brother, and dog Lucky. She enjoys being with her friends, dancing, reading, writing, and of course, playing soccer. She would like to thank Cher McClintock for being an inspirational teacher and friend, who created the opportunity for her first story to be published. carolinemilleson@hotmail.com

KATHLEEN M. MULDOON has been writing for the past twenty years. She is the author of a picture book, *Princess Pooh,* and is a frequent contributor to juvenile and adult periodicals. When not writing, she is active in church and community groups. An amputee, she also advocates for persons with disabilities through writing and public speaking. She loves cats, and treasures the antics and wet-nose kisses of her kitty Prissy. mink@texas.net

LORELEI PEPE became an artist after working in the corporate world for more than twenty-five years. She is the creator of Lorelei's Mermaids—original, handmade, whimsical mermaids made out of clay. As both artist and salesperson, she travels the local craft circuit and also showcases the mermaids in a store in Miami where she resides. A former New Yorker, and graduate of the Fashion Institute of Technology, she also "dabbles" in writing, another lifelong dream. She is currently writing angel-type stories. (305) 387-1950

CINDY POTTER and her husband Dan share their lives with their three dogs Windy Rose, Ozzie, and Kimo and cat Peanut. During their twenty-seven-year marriage, they have rescued then found the homes of or found new homes for over two hundred stray animals. Dazy Joy was their first stray dog and she enriched their lives for sixteen and a half years. (503) 788-0869

FELICE R. PRAGER is a freelance writer from Scottsdale, Arizona. After successful careers in education and retail management, she threw in the towel a few years ago to do what she loves best: write. Her work has since appeared in a number of national and local publications, as well as in a number of ezines. www.1derfulwords.com. FelPrager@aol.com

MARGARET C. PRICE is an attorney and a Northwestern theater graduate. She writes scripts and novels with the intent of uplifting the human spirit. Her writings focus on spiritual journeys. A member of the Writers Guild, she has sold scripts for both film and television; she studied screenwriting at the University of London and the American Film Institute in Los Angeles. Most recently, she has written and performed one-woman dramatizations about spirited Southern women. Her award-winning presentation of *Distant Voices,* a portrait of Susan Clay (1863), brought to life the visionary daughter-in-law of Henry Clay. She and her husband Gary and live in Lexington, Kentucky, with their three daughters. (859) 263-8131

LISA ROBERTSON began writing at the urging of her parents, who believed they saw a bit of talent in her holiday newsletters. After fifteen years of working in the veterinary field, she is now a stay-at-home mom, writing stories of her life experiences and those of her two children. Along with her husband and kids, she shares her life with four cats, and a work-in-progress English garden at her Pacific Northwest home. b4bastet@juno.com

RUTH ROCKER is a part-time Personnel Manager and former Director of the YMCA Adult Literacy Program in New Orleans.

She and her husband, Henry, have seven children, one special angel, and seventeen grandchildren. Christianity is an integral part of her life, and she currently fills the role of Granny for Granny's Angels, a group of young people dedicated to performing Christian service in the community. She recently moved from a large metropolitan area to a small rural community outside the city, where her dream is to pursue her inspirational writings. rrocker@i-55.com

LEIGH SENTER has had four short stories published in literary magazines. She has had dozens of poems and pen-and-ink drawings published in magazines as varied as *Lonzie's Fried Chicken*, *Sow's Ear Poetry Review*, and *Limestone Circle*. *The Urban Hiker* occasionally prints her thoughts on everything from diets to religion. She lives in Purnell Crossroads, North Carolina, with two teenaged daughters, Doc Watson the dog, and several goldfish.

ALAINA SMITH is a writer. Although her jobs have included newspaper editor, training coordinator, and office manager, fiction writing will always be her primary passion. Working on her novel and composing short stories keep her busy, and her loving and supportive husband Frank keeps her inspired. writersmith@yahoo.com

KATIE SNYDER has dedicated the majority of her young adulthood to traveling the world. Her adventures abroad have taken her through Southeast Asia, India, Australia, New Zealand, the South Pacific, Europe, Northern Africa, and Central America. She has a passion for traveling and has learned to "expect many miracles" from her various experiences globetrotting. She hopes to inspire and motivate others to follow their souls and seek out their dreams through writing and public speaking. (952) 890-3075. ktsnyd@iwon.com

KIRSTEN SNYDER is an eighth-grade student at Lincoln Middle School in Cottage Grove, Oregon, where she lives with her mom and dad and younger brother Sean. She enjoys writing short stories, drawing and sketching, creating greeting cards, and being with her family. Besides raising guide dogs for the blind, her passion is ice skating. She is currently training for freestyle figure-skating competition with her coach Cindy. (541) 942-2022. ksnyder@lane.k12.or.us

SHEILA STEPHENS is an international-award-winning poet, writing teacher, columnist, and speaker who enjoys helping people build their lives "from the inside out." To her, self-esteem is a spiritual journey of accepting the seed of love that divine spirit places in each heart. She's just completed *Light Up Your Dreams with Love* and *Walking with the Flowers: Insights and Inspiration from a Softer Place,* both of which honor this intent. joywriters@uswest.net

KATHLEEN STURGEON started writing at the tender age of eight, when she was recruited into the Young Writer's Workshop on Anderson Air Force Base, Guam. In subsequent years, she forgot her Chamorro but remained afflicted with this serious strain of the writing bug. She has published hundreds of nonfiction articles in military newspapers and newsletters and on Web sites, along with a few short stories and poems. kat.sturgeon@juno.com

TERESA ELIZABETH TRAXLER is seventeen years old and a senior at Le Center High School in Le Center, Minnesota. She enjoys many activities, such as volleyball, track and field, drama, and jazz band. She believes that a positive attitude is one of the main components of a happy life. She would also like to thank the people who have supported her throughout her high school years and the continual support that each person generously gives. (507) 357-6542. ttrax17@hotmail.com

MELISSA SANDY VELA is currently twenty years old and lives in San Antonio, Texas. An avid writer and reader, she loves poetry but also enjoys the many other facets of the written word. She is a junior at St. Mary's University, working toward her B.A. in the field of English/communication arts. Her poetry has been published in many anthologies and journals. She aspires to work for Walt Disney Studios as an animated feature writer. She hopes to always feel the joy and tranquility writing gives her and wishes to continue to create art through the simple scribbles of her pen across paper.

MARY ZELINKA lives with her springer spaniel, Molly McGee (a.k.a. Wild Thing), in Albany, Oregon, where she is the Program Director for the Center Against Rape and Domestic Violence. There she works to empower survivors to break the cycle of abuse and to rebuild their lives free from violence. Her work has appeared in *Chocolate for a Lover's Heart* and *Chocolate for a Teen's Heart.* maryz@proaxis.com

ACKNOWLEDGMENTS

My gratitude goes to the contributors of this book for sharing their tender, true teen stories. Their willingness to reveal funny, poignant, embarrassing, and touching tales warms my heart and adds richness beyond measure to these pages. They keep me feeling young at heart.

I continue to praise my agent, Peter Miller, and his great staff. I appreciate their support and their love of *Chocolate*. To Caroline Sutton, senior editor at Fireside–Simon & Schuster, my heartfelt thanks and good wishes for her insight and ideas. To her assistant, Nicole Diamond, thanks for your enthusiasm and sweet spirit. And hugs and kisses to the entire Fireside crew, who champion *Chocolate* routinely. And to my closer-to-home administrative support team, Jan Richardson and Tamara Johnson, may all your dreams come true.

Enormous thanks to the editing expertise of Burky Achilles and Sheila Stephens. Whenever we get together, magic happens.

Eternal love to the man in my life, my husband Eric. I love all the ways he believes in *Chocolate*. Buckets of love always to our four grown sons—Pete, David, Rick, and Tim—and our daughters-in-law Amy Jane and Stephanie. My deepest gratitude to the dream makers in my life: Cindy Potter, Jody Stevenson, and Jan Hibbard, and for my forever high school pals Kathie Millett and Carol Rolph.

Thank you to all the young women who read this book. My wish for you is that you trust your good judgment as you walk through challenges and remember to see the beauty in each new day.

ABOUT THE AUTHOR

Kay Allenbaugh is the author of *Chocolate for a Woman's Soul, Chocolate for a Woman's Heart, Chocolate for a Lover's Heart, Chocolate for a Mother's Heart, Chocolate for a Woman's Spirit, Chocolate for a Teen's Soul, Chocolate for a Woman's Blessings,* and *Chocolate for a Teen's Heart.* She resides with her husband, Eric Allenbaugh (author of *Wake-Up Calls: You Don't Have to Sleepwalk Through Your life, Love or Career*), in Lake Oswego, Oregon.

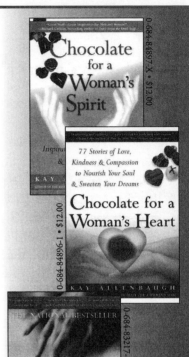